ten poems to last a lifetime

ten

poems

to

last

a

lifetime

ROGER HOUSDEN

HARMONY BOOKS
NEW YORK

Published by Harmony Books,
New York, New York.
Member of the Crown Publishing Group,
a division of Random House, Inc.
www.crownpublishing.com

Harmony Books is a registered trademark and the
Harmony Books colophon is a trademark of
Random House, Inc.

A complete list of credits for previously published
material appears at the end of the book.

Printed in the United States of America

Design by Karen Minster

Library of Congress Cataloging-in-Publication Data
Ten poems to last a lifetime / Roger
Housden.—1st ed.
Includes bibliographical references.
1. Poetry—Collections. 2. Poetry—Translations into
English. 3. Poetry—History and criticism.
I. Housden, Roger.
PN6101.T38 2004
808.81—dc22
2003023600

ISBN 1-4000-5113-4

10   9   8   7   6   5   4   3   2

First Edition

For my parents, in memoriam

"It's absurd to think that the only way to tell if a poem is lasting is to wait and see if it lasts. The right reader of a good poem can tell the moment it strikes him that he has taken a mortal wound—that he will never get over it. That is to say, permanence in poetry as in love is perceived instantly. It hasn't to await the test of time."

ROBERT FROST

Contents

9
THE ART OF DISAPPEARING
by Naomi Shihab Nye　91
You Could Tumble Any Second　93

10
THE MIND OF ABSOLUTE TRUST (Excerpt)
by Seng-Ts'an　99
It's That Simple!　101

11
WHEN DEATH COMES
by Mary Oliver　111
Amazing　113

Introduction

What is it about honey and bees that engages a beekeeper in his work for a lifetime? Or chimpanzees— Why does the primatologist Jane Goodall spend her working life alone out in Africa watching and talking to them?[1] What does a Shakespeare scholar find so fascinating about all those plays, which most of us are glad to be done with at the end of high school? And why do some people return to a few favorite poems over and over again, down through the years, when there are so many other new books and anthologies out there just waiting to be digested and absorbed?

Surely, if something, anything, is to sustain your attention, your passion, over a lifetime, it must have the capacity to reveal layers of meaning and value in ever-fresh and unexpected ways. To open your mind and heart with wonder enough to have you come back for more, and to surprise you again, and again, though each time with a different inflection or slant. It must be an unending source of discovery, of reflection, solace, and insight; of pleasure; and also of warmth and nourishment, in the way a fire can warm hands, and bread can fill the stomach.

These are some of the qualities of the eleven poems in this book. Yes, eleven. This being the last of the Ten Poems series, we thought we'd add an extra one for good measure. Each of the eleven poems is, in its own way, bread for the soul and fire for the spirit. That is why I believe they have the power to sustain our interest and attention for as long as a lifetime. They are campfires to return to over and over. Places we can go to find ourselves again, and also places that can show us things we might never have dreamed of, that can say things in language we might never have been able to quite form for ourselves.

It seems fitting that the final book is one that addresses, not so much a particular theme (*Ten Poems to Change Your Life . . . to Open Your Heart . . . to Set You Free*) as a general, overarching quality that can be found in poetry of all kinds and on every subject. It is the quality that allows great poetry itself to endure. That allows joy and delight to bubble up from the soul and tears to flow from somewhere deep down inside. Ultimately, whatever engages you for a lifetime is an expression of love. My hope for this book is that it may arouse and deepen that love in you—the love of yourself, of life, and of the world. No author can ever ask for more than that.

In literature, the quality of inexhaustibility, or timelessness, is neatly arranged under the title of "classic." And yet few of these poems, with the exception of Keats's ode "To Autumn" and Seng-Ts'an's "The Mind of Absolute Trust" are from the classical canon. They are not classics, first and foremost, because they are mostly contemporary, and so have not passed the litmus test of time.

And yet I would call them contemporary classics, because they give voice in a unique and eloquent way to timeless themes. And the force, the power of their delivery, makes them likely to hit their target, the heart of the reader, in an instant, an instant that can last forever. They also come in a language that is ours; a language that, instead of being over-lain with meanings and associations that are no longer part of our cultural experience, uses images and situations we can recognize from our daily lives.

As I have already noted in this book's epigraph, it was Robert Frost who said that

> It's absurd to think that the only way to tell if a poem is lasting is to wait and see if it lasts. The right reader of a good poem can tell the moment it strikes him that he has taken a mortal wound—that he will never get over it. That is to say, permanence in poetry as in love is perceived instantly. It hasn't to await the test of time.[2]

Every one of these poems has struck me a mortal wound. Your own list of poems "for a lifetime" is certain to be different from my own. But I doubt you will get through this book and come out unscathed.

1

MY LIFE

by Billy Collins

Sometimes I see it as a straight line
drawn with a pencil and a ruler
transecting the circle of the world

or as a finger piercing
a smoke ring, casual, inquisitive,

but then the sun will come out
or the phone will ring
and I will cease to wonder

if it is one thing,
a large ball of air and memory,
or many things,
a string of small farming towns,
a dark road winding through them.

Let us say it is a field
I have been hoeing every day,
hoeing and singing,
then going to sleep in one of its furrows,

or now that it is more than half over,
a partially open door,
rain dripping from the eaves.

Like yours, it could be anything,
a nest with one egg,
a hallway that leads to a thousand rooms—
whatever happens to float into view
when I close my eyes

or look out a window
for more than a few minutes,
so that some days I think
it must be everything and nothing at once.

But this morning, sitting up in bed,
wearing my black sweater and my glasses,
the curtains drawn and the windows up,

I am a lake, my poem is an empty boat,
and my life is the breeze that blows
through the whole scene

stirring everything it touches—
the surface of the water, the limp sail,
even the heavy, leafy trees along the shore.

Life Is a Breeze

How does he do this? I mean, write about trifles, the little moments of any ordinary day, a wry, half-smile flickering all the way through the poem, and yet at the same time manage to address something wonderful? Something, well, something that brings a deeper breath to your lungs, or that catches you off guard and takes a weight from your heart? Practically any one of his poems can stir something in you before your mind can quite decipher what it is that has affected you so. This, of course, is one of the hallmarks of great poetry. It was Wallace Stevens who once said that "poetry must resist the intelligence almost successfully."[1]

Billy Collins is a recent poet laureate of the United States, and the most widely read poet in America today. The deceptive simplicity of his work, I think, must be one of the reasons for his success, which is far greater than any other American poet since the time of Robert Frost, who was also a "poet of the people." Collins is a poet of the vernacular, of everyday speech and things, yet with a twist. His work seems so simple, so transparently obvious in its everyday concerns, that it would seem to have no interest in resisting anyone's intelligence, not even "almost." Yet it can deliver a side blow that can have you either bent double with laughter, wincing at a truth you may know but not have especially wanted to name—

The name of the author is the first to go[2]

he says, with ironic self-deprecation, in the first line of the poem "Forgetfulness"—or gasping a little for air at the sheer vision he has opened up in a single phrase or a line. And there can be times when he manages, astoundingly, to achieve all these effects at the same time.

This poem, "My Life," winds me effortlessly between its banks like a river from beginning to end, no hard knocks, no rapids, all flow and ease; yet by the time I come out at the other end something has happened; I feel different, and I don't quite know why.

All the images are from the daily round, and since he is describing his life, that may seem natural enough. But would *you* see your life

> *. . . as a straight line*
> *drawn with a pencil and a ruler*
> *transecting the circle of the world?*

So matter of fact, so deliberate and precise? So . . . geometrical? It is almost as if someone sat down and drew up a life in much the same way as you dissect a triangle. There is something so cleanly dispassionate about this image, and this is just the quality that Collins carries through so much of his work. As if he were floating slightly above the scene he is describing; or as if he were always at a certain distance from himself, noting with a certain humor the foibles and little daily rituals that fill out the texture of his life.

Distance does not necessarily imply a disconnection. On the contrary, it can give a perspective that fosters a kind of warmth, a fondness for what is being observed. And it is distance, too, that can allow us to see the humorous side of things, especially when it comes to ourselves. It was Czeslaw Milosz who said, in his poem "Love" that

> *Love means to look at yourself*
> *The way one looks at distant things*[3]

Milosz goes on in the same poem to say that it is distance that allows us to realize we are only one thing among many, and that when we see life that way, our heart is healed of ills we may not even have known we were suffering from.

So here is Billy Collins, inspecting his life, and for a moment he sees it

> *. . . as a finger piercing*
> *a smoke ring, casual, inquisitive,*

It's something of a game, blowing smoke rings, and even more of a game to try and pass your finger through it. Life can seem like that, Collins tells us; and again, whoever would have thought of such an image to describe a life?

Collins always seems to manage to come at the familiar from an odd angle, and the very oddity is awakening, somehow. I *feel* my life in a new way when taking in this image, even if I can't quite articulate what the newness is. The events, the stuff of life, are as evanescent as smoke, it suggests; and my passage through this hall of mirrors is all curiosity and wondering. Pause for a moment and consider this image for yourself, the feeling or the sensation it arouses in you, the associations it evokes from your own life's journey.

And as if to make his point, the whole image disappears in a ray of sunshine, just as the cards in a magician's hand disappear up his sleeve, and we are back in Collins's day, in which, for a moment, the sun has come out, or the phone has rung. Excuse me for a moment, let this poem look after itself for the foreseeable future, while I answer the phone, or at least contemplate its ringing tone.

Except that, when it comes to poem-making, the telephone is as fair game in Collins's mind as a smoke ring is. Anything, anything at all, is likely to work its way into one of his poems, since anything and everything is equally a part of our living world. This is it, you see, he seems to be saying. Don't think poetry and the poetic image must always come on wings from some other, transcendent world; or from deep deep down in the archeology of our unconscious. No, the visible world of pens and rulers and telephones also comes tinged with an uncommon light, should we wish to see it that way. And Collins does.

So is it one thing, or many things, your life—

> *a large ball of air and memory,*

perhaps? Here he is again, edging the familiar right up to the strange. Well, isn't it strange, to think of your life as a ball of air and memory? Strange, and perhaps disconcerting somehow? When we are very old, perhaps it is only our memories that keep us alive; that, and air—pure, thin air. But then again, his life (and ours, by implication) might equally be

> *a string of small farming towns,*
> *a dark road winding through them.*

How comforting, to think of a life this way, a series of settled communities with established traditions, all tilling the earth and sowing seeds, everything connected, given continuity, by a winding road. That the road is dark we probably take for granted, for who can expect to see where that road leads? Stanley Kunitz, the oldest poet still at work in the Western world, offers a somewhat similar image of warmth and continuity when he describes his own long life in the poem "The Layers." He speaks of the milestones receding in the distance toward the horizon,

> *and the slow fires trailing*
> *from the abandoned camp-sites,*[4]

Collins goes on to add another farming image, comparing his life to a field he has been hoeing, one in whose furrows he curls up to sleep in, which reminds me that we all make a bed of our lives to lie in. That good old farming wisdom, reaping what we sow. So many of Collins's poems let loose a cascade of images, one after the other sailing by, as if to say, if that one doesn't fit, then try this one? And so it is here, where he says of his life,

> *Like yours, it could be anything,*
> . . . .
> *so that some days I think*
> *it must be everything and nothing at once.*

And right there, in those last couple of lines, you might think him whimsical; or, instead, approaching the insight of some old Buddhist sage; or both, all at the same time. Because isn't that what the deepest wisdom is like— so simple, almost offhand, that it might pass right over your shoulder without you catching even the scent of it?

But let's not stray too far from the concrete and the quotidian: that would never do in a Billy Collins poem. So here we are, finally, this very morning, and Collins is

> *. . . sitting up in bed,*
> *wearing my black sweater and my glasses,*
> *the curtains drawn and the windows up,*

and he paints one last, beautiful picture that manages to bring together all in one scene both the physicality and the ineffability of the life that we live. He returns us to the timeless metaphor of life as breath, as wind—*ruach*, the Hebrews called it, breath-as-spirit—and it is this that pushes his poem along, and that stirs into life everything that is. This is the genius of Billy Collins, that he can lead us seamlessly from his black sweater and his glasses to the living spirit that moves across the waters and through all things.

2

ECSTASY

by Hayden Carruth

For years it was in sex and I thought
This was the most of it
                       so brief
                                a moment
or two of transport out of oneself
                             or
in music which lasted longer and filled me
with the exquisite wrenching agony
of the blues
              and now it is equally
transitory and obscure as I sit in my broken
chair that cats have shredded
by the stove on a winter night with wind and
   snow
howling outside and I imagine
the whole world at peace
                     at peace

and everyone comfortable and warm
the great pain assuaged

                              a moment
of the most shining and singular gratification.

The Great Pain Assuaged

Surely it is this, even without knowing it, that we all long for deep in our bones: *ekstasis*, the experience of being lifted out of our bodies, our pains, our sadness, and our cares, then set down, at least for a time, in a life where we are one with the current of all life, where we know that all is already well, and shall always be well. This is a poem of ecstasy, and in it, Hayden Carruth touches the peace that is not of this world, yet he does so at home, sitting in the kitchen by the stove with the wind and the snow outside. In this poem, he marries heaven with earth.

You might suspect that anyone writing a collection of poems with a title like *Scrambled Eggs and Whiskey*, in which this poem, "Ecstasy," appears, is probably someone willing to reach for the sublime in ways that are not always conventional.[1] Carruth, a social realist and a political radical, is wary of mysticism, yet his work carries some of the most penetrating insight—spiritual insight—to be found anywhere.

He was born in 1921, and published his first book when he was forty. He was, he has said, a late bloomer. Most poets thrive in their earlier years; Carruth, like his favorite malt, has only improved with age. He is the author of some thirty books, including a novel, four books of criticism, and two anthologies. *Scrambled Eggs and Whiskey* won the National Book Award in 1996 and *Doctor Jazz: Poems, 1996–2000* was published when he was eighty.[2]

For years, he lived a solitary life in the woods of northern Vermont, mixing with the local farmhands and writing about the poor and disenfranchised. Always the radical, he refused an invitation from the Clintons in 1998 to attend a millennium celebration at the White House on the grounds that Washington only served to foster the interests of those for whom poets and the poor were irrelevant. Later in his life, he took a teaching job at Syracuse, and now, despite the many honors he has received for his poetry, he lives a retirement where the small change matters.

> *For years it was in sex and I thought*
> *This was the most of it . . .*
>
> *What was in sex?*
>
> > *a moment*
> *or two of transport out of oneself*

That is to say, the temporary loss of self-consciousness that sex can offer. The brief, all too brief, release from the straitjacket of our hyperactive self-referencing, the internal monitor that keeps us forever at a certain distance, separate from life in all of its aspects. Separate from each other, from nature, from the food we eat, even, and perhaps especially, separate from ourselves.

And yet self-consciousness is no bad thing; rather, we might call it a blessing-curse. You wouldn't even have your own name without it. It is a prerequisite for the birth of individual identity, and it has thrived only in eras—in ancient Greece, among the Jews after the Diaspora, in the Italian Renaissance, and in the last four hundred years, especially in England and America—when individually was valued and recognized.[3] When the tribe or the family was the chief source of identity, the individual bore the name of his father, or was referred to as "daughter of." It was inconceivable in those times that a son would ever do anything different in the world from what his father had done. People lived in a collective rather than a personal identity.

In this light, self-consciousness is something we can be thankful for. And as it happens, Hayden Carruth's ecstasy requires no damping down of individuality or a regression to a collective state of consciousness.[4] Rather, ecstasy raises the individual to a more whole and integrated awareness, one that includes not only yourself but also others and the rest of life in general. You return from ecstatic rapture knowing you are part of a greater life, a conscious flicker in the vast network of intelligence that joins both the stars and the ants and you.

Through a deep communion with the person in whose arms you are resting, love-making can bring such ecstatic awareness. It probably allows more people access to a moment of transport out of themselves than any other medium, which is doubtless part of why it can move us so. But though you may feel groggy on getting up from the love bed, your legs shaking and tremors rippling still across your belly, it's usually not long before you are wondering about that unpaid bill, fixing something to eat, or—if you are like Hayden Carruth—taking out a pack of your favorite brand of cigarettes.

For Carruth, the ecstatic effects of music last longer. Specifically, he means jazz and the blues. Carruth has loved jazz all his life, and has said he believes the tonality and timbre of his poetry has been influenced by it. From the time of the Greek god Dionysus, music has always been a source and means of rapture, and every religious tradition makes use of it for that purpose. The first poems, after all, were odes, songs of praise to the gods.

Among the Sufis of India and Pakistan, qawwali music is the surest vehicle to join the devout to the turning of the stars.[5] The musicians play and also sing ecstatic verses from the writings of the saints. As the music reaches a crescendo, someone in the assembly may roll in ecstasy on the floor, spin like a Whirling Dervish, or rock to and fro. When the state of *wajd*, or ecstasy, is achieved, everyone present rises in its honor, and the couplet that was being sung at that moment is repeated until the ecstatic returns to waking consciousness.

What is *your* way of forgetting yourself? Of remembering something that everyday consciousness usually veils? What is it that causes your tears to flow for no reason—tears of relief, of gratitude, of sheer amazement and wonder? That brings the other world right here, like a bird on your shoulder?

I, too, have suffered the joys of music, especially the sweet other-worldliness of the Turkish *oud* and the *ney*. But it was a

work of art that stunned me for longer than anything I can re-
member. It happened the first time I went to the Museo di San
Marco, in Florence. The museum is an old monastery, and
one of the monks there was Fra Angelico, who painted each
of the monks' cells with a fresco. Today, the museum is pri-
marily dedicated to his works. They remain as they were when
they were first painted directly onto the walls of the cells.

I walked up the stone staircase to the second floor, and
when I turned to face the entrance to the monks' dormitory,
my eyes met the glow of a powerful radiance. Through the
open archway, like an apparition, "The Annunciation," Fra
Angelico's masterpiece, shone down on me from a large
stone wall. My pace immediately slowed, and within a mo-
ment or two there at the top of the stairs, my attention be-
gan to draw inward. I peered round the doorway of the first
couple of cells, and when I came to the next one, stepped in-
side. The fresco on the wall depicted the Sermon on the
Mount. The disciples were gathered in contemplation
around Jesus, who was sitting on a rock, his right arm raised,
forefinger pointing to heaven.

I stood in front of the painting entranced—by the lumi-
nous tones, lavender and green, of the disciples' robes, the
remarkable simplicity of the drawing, but above all by the
look on the faces of the disciples. They were filled with a rap-
ture that seemed both of this world and not of it at the same
time. They seemed to be showing a love for Jesus, the man,
and also for something else that could never be put into
words.

The thoughts in my mind began to ebb away. My strength

began to fail me, and I sank to the floor, unable to take my eyes from those beautiful faces. How long I sat there, I have no idea. All I know is that, when I finally got to my feet, I felt I had been filled with the love that makes the world.

Moments like these pass, but they leave a trace on the air we breathe. I do not believe we are ever quite the same again, however transitory their visitations, however completely the everyday world seems to reassert itself. Neither do they need the beauty of some Renaissance fresco, or the minor keys of esoteric music, to make themselves known to us. For Carruth, a broken chair is enough of an invitation, a chair that has been shredded by his cats, a humble seat that takes his weight by the stove as the wind and the snow howl away outside.

A doorway onto the other world can open anywhere. It has no need of anything in order to find an entry into your brain. For no reason at all, Carruth imagines

> *the whole world at peace*
> > *at peace*
> *and everyone comfortable and warm*
> the great pain assuaged . . .

When I read these lines, something in me softens, relaxes into the world. The moment is as transitory for Carruth as the ecstasy of sex was, or music; but this is no moment of personal gratification. This is more like a prayer or a naming of that which already, in some dimension, is already true, already so. What brings him joy is the experience of the world at peace, with no one left out. He is not wishing it could be so; he is experiencing the reality of it; and *that* is the ecstasy of this man who, in his long life, has known other forms of rapture, but nothing quite like this.

I wonder what arises in your mind as you read the line

the great pain assuaged

I think of it as a string of words our bones understand, even if we can't give voice to its meaning. It returns me to the pathos of separateness, the ego's constant shadow. Carruth has said in a radio interview with Tom Smith, professor of English at the University of Albany, that when the human race withdrew from the rest of the animal kingdom—perhaps around the time of the inhabitants of Lascaux and the other French caves—a great sorrow and sense of loss developed in the racial consciousness.[6] That sorrow, he feels, is still here today. We have cut away from all other species; we are on our own, not just as individuals, but as a race.

For now, though, that pain is relieved, which allows

a moment
of the most shining and singular gratification.

A moment like this is utterly unique; beyond comparison, beyond the need for any particular form: music, sex, or otherwise. It is sheer grace. It joins us, not only to the world of all living things, but also to the realms of the gods and the angels. Just one moment like this will make a lifetime worthwhile.

3

WEATHERING

by Fleur Adcock

My face catches the wind
from the snow line
and flushes with a flush
that will never wholly settle.
Well, that was a metropolitan vanity,
wanting to look young forever, to pass.
I was never a pre-Raphaelite beauty
and only pretty enough to be seen
with a man who wanted to be seen
with a passable woman.

But now that I am in love
with a place that doesn't care
how I look and if I am happy,
happy is how I look and that's all.
My hair will grow grey in any case,
my nails chip and flake,

my waist thicken, and the years
work all their usual changes.

If my face is to be weather beaten as well,
it's little enough lost
for a year among the lakes and vales
where simply to look out my window
at the high pass
makes me indifferent to mirrors
and to what my soul may wear
over its new complexion.

Happy Is How I Look

I love the unapologetic insistence on being herself that Fleur Adcock declares in this poem. She is her own woman. She is wickedly sharp, a serene pragmatist, and all in favor of common sense. Of her own development as a poet, she said, in an interview for the *Guardian* newspaper (on the publication of her *Poems 1960–2000*),

> You have to listen to your own voice. Not your heart, not your instincts, not any of that self-permissive psycho-babble stuff. No, none of that. If it was just about instincts and bright ideas it wouldn't need to be a voice. It's about words. You hear them, read them, then you write. But mostly read. Read the bloody poems.[1]

She should know, she started young. When she was seven, she wrote this:

> *The daffodils bloom at Easter-time*
> *And violets and primroses too.*
> *They cover the wood*

In a beautiful hood
Mauve and yellow and blue.

She was born in New Zealand in 1937, but when she was five her parents moved to England, and by the time she wrote the daffodil poem she had already made the English pastoral landscape her own. Her childhood ended traumatically when, in 1950, her parents took her back to New Zealand. Five years later, pregnant, and sitting her finals at Wellington University, she married an exotic, published, romantic, and successful poet. She wanted to be like him, so she married him. She had her poet but the trouble was, he had his wife. Nobody took you seriously in the fifties if you were a single woman, so there she was suddenly, pushing a pram in suburbia, bored out of her mind. You couldn't be an adult without a man then, and you couldn't be an adult with a man.

They divorced after five years. She left the first son with her husband and took their second child along with her on her first real stab at an independent life. She was a formidable Latin scholar and landed a university lectureship. The anguish and guilt of a series of affairs followed, and then she met a Crocodile Dundee character, a well-known writer of adventure stories. They married, then were divorced in five weeks, after he began slapping her around. In the divorce settlement, her husband agreed to pay her passage to England. The old country was ever alive in her imagination and this was a journey home.

She found a job as a librarian that sustained her and her

son for fifteen years and bought her a few hours of solitude each day to write in. As for marriage, she knew at twenty she would never go through it again. "Affairs, yes, relationships, no," she laughed in the same *Guardian* interview in 2000.

Some years after landing in England again, Adcock took a year off to go and live the life of a recluse in the English Lake District, home and inspiration of Wordsworth. It was during this year that she wrote "Weathering," a poem as shorn of romantic sentiment, yet as loving and warm, as you will find anywhere.

I can see her now, out in the bracing wind that blows in from Scotland and over the northern peaks, her face turned to the snow-brushed air and loving the waking life in it, loving, too, the flush of color it raises in her cheeks, a flush, she knows,

> *that will never wholly settle.*

It will never fully be gone from her cheeks because she is already of a certain age, and because she has willingly and freely chosen a life in the elements over life of *metropolitan vanity*. Not for her the morning session of makeup; rather, I imagine, a wash in cold northern water, followed by a brisk walk over the mountains in weather that could shift ten times in a day. You will never look much younger than your years in northern weather like that, though that's of no concern to Adcock, who finds herself invigorated, inspired, by the cold. "When it's frosty," she has said, "I feel like I have been taking some interesting drug."

Like most of us, however, she has known the desire *to look young forever, to pass. To pass*—to be looked over by the opposite sex, and her own sex as well, and perhaps to be considered worth a second look. She cherishes no illusions of beauty for herself and is well aware that, in her own estimation at least, she is

> *. . . only pretty enough to be seen*
> *with a man who wanted to be seen*
> *with a passable woman.*

There is no self-recrimination in these lines, no bitterness or sense of inadequacy. She is merely stating her view of herself as honestly and simply as words can convey.

But what changes during her time in the Lake District is that she falls in love, not with a man, but

> *with a place that doesn't care*
> *how I look and if I am happy, . . .*

so that now,

> *happy is how I look and that's all.*

The natural world is completely impartial to our looks and our character. It will take all the love we have to give, and give no criticism or judgment in return. And Adcock, who has fallen in love with the Lake District, feels utterly content in being herself there. After all, the more we live our days in love—whatever the object of our love may be—the more complete and whole we feel.

While she attributes this shift to her love of the rugged landscape alone, she also implies, although without naming it, the part played by solitude in her happy state. She is up there among the fells and the cold streams all on her own, and her solitude brings her close to herself in a way that allows her muses to sing verses in her ear. This poem is just one of the many that poured from the end of her pen there among the dales. Fleur Adcock has sung the praises of solitude in other poems, most famously in "Against Coupling." Savor the sardonic humor of the first few lines:

> *I write in praise of the solitary act:*
> *of not feeling a trespassing tongue*
> *forced into one's mouth, one's breath*
> *smothered, nipples crushed against the*
> *ribcage. . . .*[2]

But do not think she is some man-hater, harboring only disillusion because of her early experiences of marriage. No, her time in the Lake District was not a flight from relationship, it was a return to herself. Relationship and solitude do not have to be mutually exclusive. Other poems of hers, such as "Tokens," reveal a deep intimacy with men.

> *The sheets have been laundered clean*
> *of our joint essence—a compound,*
> *not a mixture; but here are still*

your forgotten pipe and tobacco,
your books open on my table,
your voice speaking in my poems.[3]

In "Weathering," though, she is at home with herself, and entirely at ease with the fact that

. . . the years
work all their usual changes.

This is not the conventional wisdom of an age in which jogging and gym memberships are de rigueur. It is less common now to accept physical change with such nonchalance. We harbor the notion, rather, that our physical future is in our own hands, and that there is little that a good skin cream, yoga, or free weights can't do. Failing that, there is always botox, silicon, and the surgeon's knife.

Adcock, on the other hand, is more than happy to exchange

. . . a year among the lakes and vales

for a ruddy complexion. A sustained receptivity to the natural world can do this—it can make us more aware, more accepting of our transient state. Branches break, after all, and leaves fall. A dead crow will lie without ceremony just beyond your front door. The natural passage of the seasons, of life and death, can help us make peace with the sagging that time brings, and our own inevitable fall from the tree, in the light of which we may even forget to notice a thickening waistline.

Finally, consider these last few lines, in which she tells us that

> *. . . simply to look out my window*
> *at the high pass*
> *makes me indifferent to mirrors . . .*

She begs the question of us, her readers: To what degree are we, ourselves, enslaved to the mirror? The tyranny of the mirror is almost universal in Western culture, and especially for women. Yet Adcock, in this poem, is free of the mirror's power. She is at home with herself, just as she is, and needs no second opinion. That's why it is enough for her to know that happy is how she looks, and that's all. Perhaps, when we come home to ourselves at last in the way Fleur Adcock has done in this poem, we shall see beyond the dry skin, the crow's feet, the graying hair. We shall come to understand, finally, what Derek Walcott means when he says in his poem "Love After Love":

> *Peel your image from the mirror.*
> *Sit. Feast on your life.*[4]

4

SUNSET

by Rainer Maria Rilke

Slowly the west reaches for clothes of new colors
which it passes to a row of ancient trees.
You look, and soon these two worlds both leave you,
one part climbs toward heaven, one sinks to earth,

leaving you, not really belonging to either,
not so hopelessly dark as that house that is silent,
not so unswervingly given to the eternal as that thing
that turns to a star each night and climbs—

leaving you (it is impossible to untangle the threads)
your own life, timid and standing high and growing,
so that, sometimes blocked in, sometimes reaching out,
one moment your life is a stone in you, and the next, a star.

—TRANSLATED BY ROBERT BLY

Living in Two Worlds

The image that opens this poem by Rilke has come over the ocean to America with me, and lives on in my mind as it has for years. Three miles out of Bath, in England, going north, the winding road dips down and then back up to face a row of tall beech trees standing clear against the sky on the top of Windy Hill. Countless times I have passed that way in the late afternoon, the sun dropping away to the west over Wales, lighting the beeches against the sky and throwing their row of shadows down over the hill. Sometimes, I would stop the car and watch, there in the falling light, as one world gave way to the next, the day to the night, the earth to the heavens. And yet, as Seamus Heaney says in his poem "Postscript":

> *Useless to think you'll park and capture it*
> *More thoroughly. You are neither here nor there,*
> *A hurry through which known and strange things pass*
> *As big soft buffetings come at the car sideways*
> *And catch the heart off guard and blow it open.*[1]

Sunset and sunrise are in-between times, when two worlds overlap and anything is possible. It used to be said that this was the time when the folk from the other world—the fairies, the elves, and also the dead—would slip through the veil and become visible for those with the eyes to see. Membranes, both physical and mental, are permeable then to invisible forces, visitors from the inner as well as from the outer worlds. Perhaps this is why so many artists of the Romantic and Impressionist eras—Turner, especially, and also Monet—painted so many sunsets. It was the light they were interested in, of course, but it was surely also the magic, the wonder of that particular time of day that they succeeded in expressing in their work.

This poem by Rilke was first published in his second book, *Das Büch der Bilder,* translated variously as *The Book of Images, The Book of Paintings,* or (per Robert Bly) *The Book of Pictures.*[2] Bly, whose translation I am using here, has said that Rilke was intending with this book to write in a painterly way, using some of the disciplines of painting. Rilke, who was in his mid-twenties, was living in Paris at the time, and was married to Clara Westhoff, a student of Rodin, the famous sculptor. Rodin would urge the young poet to go off to the zoo and ob-serve the animals there, to pay close attention to the physical world, and to engage in a degree of objectivity that would trust the eyes and the ears as well as the subjective life of the soul. Rilke heeded the old sculptor; he turned his gaze out-ward and came to be a master of the poetic image of the liv-ing world much as an artist learns to capture objects in paint.

This is why the first image in this poem seems so familiar to me. The trees and the sunset are not in his imagination alone. Rilke has been there; he has watched the evening drama unfold; he has seen that line of trees, just as you and I may have done. The physical image is the foundation for all the associations that make up the rest of the poem. Like Cezanne with his apples, Rilke draws on the natural world to evoke sensations that ripple through our body of memory as well as our imagination. In his *Book of Pictures*, Rilke opens the door onto a large room full of word paintings and ushers his readers in.

In the daily pageant of sunset, one world is exchanged for another, and Rilke captures exactly the pathos of the human predicament in the line,

> *leaving you, not really belonging to either,*

We are not creatures of darkness only, not solitary and silent as that house on the hill may seem at the approach of dusk. And yet we are not angels either, *unswervingly given to the eternal.* Where *do* we belong, exactly? The question would not even arise if we had both feet firmly in either this world or the next. But as humans, we occupy what seems to be an intermediate realm somewhere between the two.

The trees and the animals know where they belong. The question of belonging does not arise for them, which is why the use of animal analogies for the human condition has never made sense to me. When Jesus says that the birds of the air have no worry for the morning, or for where they will rest their heads, what has that got to do with you and me? We are *not*, after all, beasts of the field or birds of the air. Life would be far less complicated if we were. But we have the small matter of self-consciousness to contend with; the capacity for self-awareness and self-reflection that pigs and horses, to my knowledge, do not share with us. And we probably have a great deal more self-consciousness now than we ever did two thousand years ago. Hence our restlessness and uncertainty.

Neither are we angels. Nor, I suspect, have most of us ever been. We are spared that luxury also. A purely angelic response to life might be to live from the premise that everything, no matter what, is all right, whatever may be happening in the world of contingencies.

> *And all shall be well and*
> *All manner of thing shall be well*[3]

says T. S. Eliot, in "Little Gidding," borrowing the thought from a medieval saint, Julian of Norwich.[4] Part of us, I think, intuits the truth in Julian's (and Eliot's) sentiment. There is a deep faith in the process of life that we can know as human beings. And yet we are buffeted constantly by the winds of fortune, and there are too many days, weeks, years even, when it doesn't *feel* as though everything is all right at all.

We live, then, in two worlds, not quite belonging to either,

> *leaving you (it is impossible to untangle the threads)*
> *your own life, timid and standing high and growing,*

There is something wonderful in these two lines. Rilke is simple and honest about his experience. He is neither full of optimism about his life, nor is he defeated by it. He gives voice to the fragility and also the fortitude that a human being can know, often in the same moment. As if the essence of a human being is defined, not by one of two polarities, hope or despair, limit or possibility, but by a third quality that embraces them both. We are truly human, perhaps, when we find ourselves willing to live the paradox of our nature (*timid and standing high*) made as we are of both clay and light.

Then, two lines that take my breath away. They name my experience exactly:

> *so that, sometimes blocked in, sometimes reaching out,*
> *one moment your life is a stone in you, and the next, a star.*

These last lines echo on in my mind long after I have put away the book. Because I know the stone, I know the star. And because, at times, I can sense a third thing that these lines are pointing toward: a quality of simplicity and freedom that can acknowledge and embrace both ends of the spectrum at once. This is why Rilke's poem, like few others I have ever read, captures in perfect pitch the essence of what it means, and also what it feels like, to be truly human.

5

FOR THE SAKE
OF STRANGERS

by Dorianne Laux

No matter what the grief, its weight,
we are obliged to carry it.
We rise and gather momentum, the dull strength
that pushes us through crowds.
And then the young boy gives me directions
so avidly. A woman holds the glass door open,
waits patiently for my empty body to pass through.
All day it continues, each kindness
reaching toward another—a stranger
singing to no one as I pass on the path, trees
offering their blossoms, a retarded child
who lifts his almond eyes and smiles.
Somehow they always find me, seem even
to be waiting, determined to keep me
from myself, from the thing that calls to me
as it must have once called to them—
this temptation to step off the edge
and fall weightless, away from the world.

Back from the Edge

This poem is a tribute to the survival of the human spirit in the face of all adversity, to our capacity to continue living even when it would seem easier to lie down forever and let life go on without us. It is a tribute, too, to the way we can support one another unknowingly through the smallest, apparently insignificant of acts. It is a reminder that anything and everything can matter in this world in which everyone is joined through the current of life to everyone else.

> *No matter what the grief, its weight,*
> *we are obliged to carry it.*

A failed relationship, a death in the family, the loss of our livelihood, the loss of our health, loneliness: If they have not done so already, one or more of these events will come to all of us sooner or later. Or perhaps no such calamity has touched your life, and your spirit is heavy for no apparent reason. For no reason at all, there can be long periods when life can seem not worth living. And yet, for the great majority of us, the sheer will to survive, to go on, will prevail over the wish to take our own life and be apparently free of it all for ever.

We rise and gather momentum, the dull strength
that pushes us through crowds.

The dull strength: It's true, how dulling depression is, yet something in us can take over, click into automatic, push one foot in front of the other, despite ourselves. We trudge through life like a ghost in times like these. Dorianne Laux captures it exactly in these four lines of her poem, and rescues the feeling from any hint of shame. Neither afraid nor ashamed of her feelings, however socially unacceptable they may be, she has obviously been down there, in that dark dank hole.

And she has also climbed out, no doubt more than once. A single mother with a family history of violence and abuse, she did every kind of casual labor, from being a gas station manager to a doughnut holer. Then, when she was thirty, she moved from her home state of Maine to the west coast, where, supported by scholarships and grants, she graduated with a B.A. degree in English. Her first book of poetry, *Awake*, was published in 1990 and nominated for the Bay Area Book Reviewers Award.[1] "This is a poetry of risk," Philip Levine wrote of Laux's first collection; "it will go to the very edge of extinction to find the hard facts that need to be sung." He could have been speaking of this poem, "For the Sake of Strangers," which is to be found in her second collection, *What We Carry*—itself a finalist for the National Book Critics Circle Award.[2] Since then, she has been awarded various prizes and fellowships and has become an associate professor of creative writing at the University of Oregon. Poetry, and the poetic vision, have remade Dorianne Laux.

Laux writes, she has said (in a web interview for *Perihelion*), "for the ones who are unable to write, for the heroes of my life: my family, my friends, the woman on the corner with a baby on one hip and a bag of groceries on the other, the child rapt in her joy, the man standing on his porch smoking a cigarette and feeling useless. I don't do this because I'm a great humanitarian, I simply can't help writing about these people—I see myself in them. And what I want most is to communicate to them that I have seen them standing there, and how, exactly, they have moved me. I am not ashamed of my love for them, or my pity, or my fear." These are the people who fill this poem; a poem that is, in essence, one of gratitude.

Ten years or so ago, my wife's daughter Hannah died of cancer just before her fourth birthday. In her book, *Hannah's Gift*, Maria tells the story of the lessons she was taught on her way through that fire.[3] After Hannah's death, Maria writes, "it was as if I had been lowered into a vat of slow-drying cement; I had become immobile gradually, and now felt almost completely paralyzed by grief." A few months later, she was standing by the side of the road.

"By the sound of its engine, I knew the car was coming fast. I stood on the curb, and with a sense of calm detachment, rolled the image around in my mind. Before the unsuspecting speeder could slam on his brakes, I would throw myself in front of him. . . . A white sedan crested the hill and roared past. I turned my head and closed my eyes as a whirl of dust blew into my face. My body started to shake. Stepping back from the curb, I collapsed in a heap on the grass."

Gradually, Maria came back from the edge, began to notice again the ripeness of melons in the market, laughed out loud at a joke, or bent down to wipe a scuff mark from the toe of her shoe. Then, within sixteen months of Hannah's death, she had given birth to two more daughters, Margaret and Madelaine. Her son, Will,

> had learned to read, Margaret had walked, Claude [Maria's husband at the time] had raised money for cancer research, and Madelaine had swallowed her first gulp of the world. I no longer felt willing for life to continue on without me. . . . The grief that once threatened to swallow me up had found a home in my bones. My suffering wasn't something I was going to have to let go of; it had become part of what I had to offer, part of who I am.

The world had called to Maria, and she had responded. As Dorianne Laux responds in this poem.

> *And then the young boy gives me directions*
> *so avidly. A woman holds the glass door open,*
> *waits patiently for my empty body to pass through.*
> *All day it continues, each kindness*
> *reaching toward another . . .*

There is a tiny gap in Laux's depression, the smallest aperture that allows her to look up and notice what, on an even darker day, would be hidden from her eyes: that the world goes on; that life is full to the brim in the person of a young boy; that generosity, kind-heartedness, is still at large in the world, in the person of a woman who does something as small and yet as significant as holding a door open for her *empty body to pass through.*

Something similar once happened to me in, of all places, the Sinai desert.[4] I was traveling on foot with two guides and their camels through the great stretches of silence and sand. We had been traveling for a week already, and the emptiness of the desert had begun seeping into my mind and imagination. My own life felt empty. My feet were sore, my legs were aching, the wind was whipping through me. Was this what I wanted? Plodding head down through a bare and featureless land for no other reason than for the sake of it. Fear was already at my elbow; it filtered in with the awareness of my limited resources and how easily I could be swept from existence.

We pushed on for hours until we finally reached the far side of a great plain. Selman, one of my guides, had gone on ahead, and we caught sight of him now in the distance. He was crouching by a fire among some rocks below us. He had already made camp and hobbled the camels. We clambered down to join him, my legs barely holding. I threw all the clothes in the bag on my back and lay down by the flames like a child, teeth chattering, vital force gone. Selman took his only blanket and gently covered me with it. I mumbled some thanks.

"We are all brothers in the desert," he said, without affectation. I felt tears well up as I took in our simple human kinship. No great emotion, the passing of a blanket and a cup of tea. Our shared human frailty, the ceaseless wandering together on the road from birth to death, and maybe beyond.

Of course you don't need to go to the desert to know kindness like this: A stranger calls to Laux in her poem, merely through the song that she is singing to no one. Even the trees speak to her, offering her their blossoms; a retarded child smiles. The whole world is speaking, if only we can listen, even for a moment. The whole world is trying always to find us, to rescue us from ourselves, from our own self-absorption; from the despair that lives in everything and everyone. From

> *this temptation to step off the edge*
> *and fall weightless, away from the world.*

It is not empathy that Laux is seeking in this poem, it is immersion. She is asking us to immerse ourselves in the full experience of our humanity. In this beautiful elegy of hope and gratitude, Dorianne Laux listens to the big breathing world, and steps back from the edge willing to bear the weight of her own pain and the gravity of existence. The world calls, and she responds. She returns from the brink willing to affirm the worth of her own life. Remember, finally, what Mary Oliver says in her poem "Wild Geese": that

> *Whoever you are, no matter how lonely,*
> *the world offers itself to your imagination,*
> *calls to you like the wild geese, harsh and exciting—*
> *over and over announcing your place*
> *in the family of things.*[5]

6

SONG OF A MAN WHO HAS COME THROUGH

by D. H. Lawrence

Not I, not I, but the wind that blows through me!
A fine wind is blowing the new direction of Time.
If only I let it bear me, carry me, if only it carry me!
If only I am sensitive, subtle, oh, delicate,
   a winged gift!
If only, most lovely of all, I yield myself and
   am borrowed
By the fine, fine wind that takes its course through
   the chaos of the world
Like a fine, an exquisite chisel, a wedge-blade inserted;
If only I am keen and hard like the sheer tip of a wedge
Driven by invisible blows,
The rock will split, we shall come at the wonder,
   we shall find the Hesperides.

Oh, for the wonder that bubbles into my soul,
I would be a good fountain, a good well-head,
Would blur no whisper, spoil no expression.

What is the knocking?
What is the knocking at the door in the night?
It is somebody wants to do us harm.

No, no, it is the three strange angels.
Admit them, admit them.

The Knock at Your Door

D. H. Lawrence's message in this poem is urgent, an exhortation to wake up to a truer life while there is yet time. The true life, for Lawrence, runs counter to the tame and comfortable existence that passes for contentment among the middle classes, the bourgeois society that Lawrence, son of a miner, was always suspicious of, and, despite his status as a writer, an outsider to. It also runs counter to the certainties of religious dogma, even though Lawrence was a deeply religious poet. For Lawrence had a religion all of his own, one that was constructed, not on theories or concepts, but on the basis of pure, passionate, lived experience.

D. H. Lawrence is as much prophet as poet, one who called the attention of his and future generations to the deeper life that runs always below the surface of the individual personality. Though he is better known today as a novelist, and especially for the once controversial *Lady Chatterley's Lover*, his first published works (in 1909) were poems, and his collected poetic works amount to one of the most vital and innovative contributions to twentieth-century literature.[1]

Joyce Carol Oates has said that if you read Lawrence's poems as a complete body of work, they can be seen as "a kind of mystical appropriation of his life, or *life itself,* in which the essential sacredness of 'high and low', 'beauty' and 'ugliness', 'poetry' and 'non-poetry' " is celebrated in a way that entirely transcends dualistic notions of right or wrong, good or bad. Yes, indeed. This is why Lawrence was a prophet: He was always leaping over and beyond received wisdom, beyond cultural conformity, beyond the collective dreams of wealth and celebrity, to a radical vision of life that transcended ordinary values; a vision that welcomed the dark along with the light, and celebrated the world of the senses as the living God.

The title of this poem, "Song of a Man Who Has Come Through," hints at resurrection, a theme that recurs throughout Lawrence's work. And from the very first line he suggests that renewal is not something we can just do for ourselves. It is not an act of will; it does not require the application of this or that technique.

> *Not I, not I, but the wind that blows through me!*
> *A fine wind is blowing the new direction of Time.*
> *If only I let it bear me, carry me, if only it carry me!*

It is intuition, and also instinct, that can let us feel and hear the wind he is speaking of. It is nothing less than the breath of the Holy Spirit, which moves not only each of us as individuals, but the culture as a whole, in ways we may never have suspected to be its doing. God is not some anthropomorphic daddy sitting somewhere invisible; He is the living breath, the *pneuma,* that moves through all things. That IS all things. The words for breath, wind, and soul commingle in

every language. In this respect, Lawrence is in the grand tra-
dition of Walt Whitman, who said

> *I inhale great draughts of space,*
> *The east and the west are mine, and the north and the*
>   *south are mine.*[2]

Emily Dickinson said it this way:

> *Inebriate of Air—am I—*[3]

And John Masefield, a near contemporary of Lawrence's,
could have been summarizing his fellow Englishman's entire
religious view when he wrote that

> *There is no God, but we, who breathe the air,*
> *Are God ourselves and touch God everywhere.*[4]

This *fine wind* is blowing not just through Lawrence himself,
but is also *blowing the new direction of Time.* It is ushering in a
new possibility in human affairs and society. But it is a *fine*
wind, so you and I need to adjust our senses to it; we need to
be *sensitive, subtle,* if we are to register its presence and allow its
influence. The same is true for the culture in general. Law-
rence knows that he must open himself to the invisible cur-
rent, yield to its touch, if it is to enter his life. It requires an
attitude of alert receptivity to what is beyond the rational mind.

And yet this wind is also like *an exquisite chisel, a wedge-blade
inserted.* It has teeth. It can cut like a knife through chaos, get

to the point, which is truth, without mincing words. And
Lawrence, too, wants this same quality for himself. He, too,
wants to be *keen and hard,* the hard tip of a wedge

> *Driven by invisible blows,*

As if the sharpness of his intention were honed and also
driven down deep by the insistence of this same fine wind
that he yields himself to, down into the rock. And what is this
rock, if not the hard heart that remains unmoved at our cen-
ter? I am reminded of a comment by another contemporary
of Lawrence, the Sufi sage Hazrat Inayat Khan, who said that
the heart is a rock, and can be broken open only by another
rock.[5] And these lines of Rilke:

> *To praise is the whole thing! A man who can praise*
> *comes toward us like ore out of the silences*
> *of rock. . . .*[6]

Which is an echo of Lawrence, when he says:

> *The rock will split, we shall come at the wonder, we*
> *shall find the Hesperides.*

When the heart bursts open and lets in the flood of life, *we
shall come at the wonder.* What a beautiful phrase that is! But
more than that, what a beautiful possibility. The Hesperides
is the legendary garden in the Far West of the world where
golden apples grow. When the rock in us splits open wide,

then we shall come upon our own fabled garden, which was there all along. This is what Lawrence has said elsewhere about wonder, which is nothing other than praise:

> How can one save one's soul? One can only *live* one's soul. The business is to live, really live. And this needs wonder. And what is wonder? A natural religious sense.

The next three lines of his poem are almost a prayer.

> *Oh, for the wonder that bubbles into my soul,*
> *I would be a good fountain, a good well-head,*
> *Would blur no whisper, spoil no expression.*

It is the fountain that breaks from the rock, an ancient image for the Blessed Virgin, the new life. And he prays to be a good fountain, one that will not distort the truth of what these rising waters need to bring into the world.

And then comes the fear, the inevitable backlash of the ego in the face of the unknown, in the face of the darkness:

> *What is the knocking at the door in the night?*
> *It is somebody wants to do us harm.*

How strange it is, this immediate impulse to imagine the worst, a faint shadow, perhaps, of the fear of death, a trace of the primal fear that lives in us all. But in Lawrence's poem, another, firmer voice rises above the fear:

No, no, it is the three strange angels.
Admit them, admit them.

This is the still small voice of unmistakable authority. Something in us knows that another life is possible, that a larger life is knocking at our door. *The three strange angels*—I think the angels are strange, unknown to us, because they do not represent the old religious orthodoxy. All angels are messengers, but these three are the messengers of a new dispensation. They are calling us to a new life, the taste of which may be on our tongue, but the name for which has yet to surface in our language.

And are these angels deep inside our own heart, knocking to be let out, or outside of us waiting to be let in? Both directions, of course, carry a symbolic weight; and there is no reason why Lawrence might not be alluding to the possibility that grace, transcendent help, comes from the two directions at once. Yet with his emphasis throughout his life and work on the creative, transcendent power that lies in each of us, I would take these strange angels to be knocking, even now, at this very moment, to be set free from the inner recesses of our own hearts. The new dispensation, the religious impulse of this immediate moment, presses to come forth from us, not from some messiah, whether in the past or the future. It is knocking on your door and mine. May we live, you and I, in such a way as to be the good fountain, the good well-head, that would send forth that wonder.

7

LYING IN A HAMMOCK AT WILLIAM DUFFY'S FARM IN PINE ISLAND, MINNESOTA

by James Wright

Over my head, I see the bronze butterfly,
Asleep on the black trunk,
Blowing like a leaf in green shadow.
Down in the ravine behind the empty house,
The cowbells follow one another
Into the distances of the afternoon.
To my right,
In a field of sunlight between two pines,
The droppings of last year's horses
Blaze up into golden stones.
I lean back as the evening darkens and comes on.
A chicken hawk floats over, looking for home.
I have wasted my life.

This Is It

The clarity of every image in this poem is made possible, or at least given room, by the horizontal position Wright has taken down there on William Duffy's farm in Minnesota. When was the last time you or I lay prone in a hammock, head lolled lazily this way or that, eyes resting with ease on whatever happens to be in our line of sight?

I can't remember the last time I lay in a hammock. I can feel the rough rope around my shoulders and beneath my hipbone, and I can see the color, blue, of the twine. But where was it, and who was I with? Just writing those words brings it all back. We were in Mexico, my wife and I, on the edge of a lagoon on the Yucatán coast. We were on a winter vacation, and the hammock was the only thing we bickered about. Whose turn it was.

Lying in a hammock is the perfect metaphor for the willingness to do nothing, nothing at all. To forego all duties and responsibilities, to lie back and let go. I wonder if the reason we allow ourselves so little of this luxury is that we are afraid we and our lives would slip through our fingers; that without the rod so many of us have made for our backs, we would turn into jelly, devoid of all will. Our culture is so fixated on the necessity for *doing* that if we are idle for a while, we are very likely to have the thought that we are wasting our lives.

Good Protestants that we are, that must undoubtedly be the most cardinal of sins. It is no accident that a recent *New York Times* best-seller was called *What Should I Do with My Life?*[1] Everybody wants to "have a life," or "get a life," and that usually means throwing yourself into some gainful activity. Above all, it means being productive and generating income. So lazing around in a hammock is pretty low on our list of cultural values. If you love to rest, and do nothing, you are either sick or a loser. At the head of the power lunch and ahead of the game, that's where you need to be.

James Wright saw life differently. Look at these few lines from a poem he called "A Prayer to Escape the Market Place":

> *I renounce the blindness of the magazines.*
> *I want to lie down under a tree.*
> *This is the only duty that is not death.*[2]

The desire to make art an alternative to the reality that surrounded him as a young man growing up in Ohio runs like a river through his whole body of work. An alternative reality in which beauty matters, and where there is a true compassion for the suffering of the world. Wright was born in 1927 and witnessed his father work all his life in the Hazel-Atlas Glass factory, except when, during the lean times of the Depression, he was frequently laid off.

The family lived under the constant threat of poverty and in an industrial landscape that gave Wright some firsthand experience of Blake's "dark satanic mills." His whole life was marked by an urgency never to follow in his father's footsteps, and literature and poetry were to be the materials from which he would make his own world. Not that he wished to deny his origins—his work is full of the low-life characters of his hometown of Martin's Ferry—rather, his art gave him the means to refashion his own experience; it was a vehicle for the free and natural expression of his feeling, for his utter delight in language, and for his love of the natural world.

He joined the army when he was eighteen, and it was through the GI Bill that he got his college education at Kenyon College, the most literary place in the state of Ohio. He went on to live the life of a college professor, though not unmarked by his wild and sometimes manic character. He was fired from the University of Minnesota for missing classes and for getting into barroom fistfights, all the result of excessive drinking. Then he won a Guggenheim Fellowship, and in 1966 landed a post at Hunter College, in New York City, where he remained until his death in 1980.

Like many Northerners—like myself—Wright had a lifelong love affair with Italy and the south of France. He and his second wife, Annie, would spend their summers in one or the other country, and as often as he could, Wright would take a term away from teaching to travel there slowly from town to town reveling in the pace, the climate, and, yes, the pleasures of laziness and love. Wright was not at heart a

Protestant soul, and the image of the hammock is an echo of his love for the Mediterranean idyll—a South of the mind, even more than a geographical location. An environment, a way of being and seeing, that can be a healing balm for those in whom the seriousness of the North is ingrained from birth. Dozens of his poems bear the names and the mark of that sun-drenched world, one that lived as much in his imagination as in fact—which makes it no less real.

> *The Mediterranean, nearer to the moon*
> *Than this mountain is,*
> *Shines.*[3]

Look at all those *b*'s in the first three lines of "Lying in a Hammock." How full-lipped, how bountiful this letter is; how it blossoms on the mouth over and again in these lines. As if to remind us how blessed we are, simply to be able to look up over our head and drink down the beauty of nature whenever we think of it. The colors, all bronze, black, and green; the tremor of movement in the *blowing*, and even the butterfly feeling safe enough to sleep.

The next image takes us from seeing to hearing, to the cowbells down in the ravine. But it takes us as well out into the larger picture, in which there is an *empty house*, and—that beautiful phrase—*the distances of the afternoon*. That word *empty* sends a little tremor through me, I'm not sure why. It returns me somehow to that particular sense of presence, of aliveness one can feel when one is all alone in nature. And the *distances*—I think of the layers of haze, of different densities, that can sometimes stretch away into a late summer afternoon. I wonder what images these words evoke in you.

The third image, placed precisely *between two pines,* to the poet's *right,* is a beautiful redemption of the most humble matter. Horse droppings blazing in the sun like *golden stones.* Everything and anything can assume a radiant light, Wright is saying, when you look at it with innocent eyes, eyes free of concern and worry, of thoughts of the past or the future. When you are here, fully here, the world is in its fullness also. This is when even the stones—even horse dung—will speak. This is when you are truly alive.

Then, as the evening begins to take away the visible world, a last fleeting image of the chicken hawk heading for home, and finally, that shocking, entirely unexpected last line:

> *I have wasted my life.*

There I was, in the hammock alongside him, feeling with him the reverberations of those images of beauty, tasting the honey of them on my tongue, seeing those *golden stones,* and then this last line. A line that jolts me out of my idyll. That shocks me awake to a greater aliveness still, awake to a sensation, below words, of the complexity, the beauty, the tensions, that make up my life.

Wright was a lifelong admirer and student of the work of Rilke, and the ghost of Rilke's poem "Archaic Torso of Apollo" can be felt just beneath the surface of this poem by Wright. Rilke's poem describes the beauty of an ancient Greek sculpture, a headless torso of Apollo. The beauty of the stone body is almost blinding, and it seems to emit a light the way a star does. Then, suddenly, after the image of the star, Rilke ends the poem with these lines:

> . . . . . . *for there is no place at all*
> *that isn't looking at you. You must change your life.*[4]

The same shocking, awakening last sentence; the same call to another life, one deeper, more alive perhaps, than the mere lull of beauty.

So what is Wright saying? That lying in a hammock in the embrace of beauty can be just another way of falling asleep to a sharper, more passionate life that is possible for us? Or that the relaxed state of ease, in contrast to our more usual busyness and preoccupation, is precisely what is needed in order to awaken to ourselves more deeply? I don't know. The ambiguity, the puzzlement, the ripples of that last line, add dramatically to the power of the poem. What do you think?

Common wisdom says that anyone who idles about in a hammock is wasting his life away. Perhaps Wright is turning this on its head, suggesting that these few moments of seeing the world with open eyes are precisely what make his life matter. You certainly don't need to lie in a hammock to know moments like this. They can happen anywhere, at any time. And you can lie in a hammock and worry over nothing for hours. But the relaxed, open state that the hammock represents is usually a necessary condition for a moment of genuine aliveness. By inference, perhaps the rest of Wright's experience, when he is caught up in the whirl of the world, escapes his full attention, his full participation, and disappears into the mist of the past.

To my ears, this last line is not self-accusing; neither is it depressed or cynical. When I read this poem to a friend recently, she said that Wright was expecting too much of himself; that moments of seeing, of presence, come and go fleetingly for all of us. Why not embrace with gladness those moments of true aliveness you do manage to live, rather than curse yourself for all the time you might seem to have wasted in boredom, in the busyness of life's struggle, or in sheer distraction? She has a point, and Wright may even have wanted to prompt some adverse reaction like this in his reader; one that, in itself, would serve as a wake-up call and an opportunity for self-questioning. But I read the line differently.

First, it goes against the mood of the rest of the poem. Wright does this often in his work; he sets up a dynamic tension between the opposing forces of hope and despair, blossoming and breakage (this poem is in a collection called *The Branch Shall Not Break*, published in 1963). Out of the ensuing struggle, energy arises before our eyes right there in the poem. The same struggle, between feeling alive and lackluster, awake and asleep, happens in us, and what Wright's poem does is mirror that human condition.

When I read this last line, I feel chastened, not chastised. That is, some of the excess of self-importance, of self-satisfaction, is siphoned out of me. It's almost a bodily experience, a sensation of air being drawn out of my tissue. It returns me to proportion, reduces me to a truer picture of myself, but without rancor or blame.

> "What's writing really about?" asked the poet Ted
> Hughes. "It's about trying to take fuller possession
> of the reality of your life."[5]

> *I rhyme*
> *To see myself, to set the darkness echoing.*

Seamus Heaney says, in the poem "Personal Helicon."[6] This is what I believe James Wright was trying to do for himself in this poem, and this is also what he offers to you and to me. Far from being accusing, he is, without judgment, inhaling the poignant bittersweetness of his life experience, the reality of his all-too-human life. He offers us the invigorating feeling of being alive in all our complexity and fullness; not with self-recrimination, nor by analyzing his successes and failures, but in the impartial act of seeing itself. If you want the vitality, the sheer aliveness, of this poem to enter your bloodstream, then read it aloud to yourself from time to time. It may remind you of the line in Mary Oliver's poem, the one that ends this book, "When Death Comes":

> *I don't want to end up simply having visited this world.*[7]

8

TO AUTUMN

by John Keats

Season of mists and mellow fruitfulness,
    Close bosom-friend of the maturing sun;
Conspiring with him how to load and bless
    With fruit the vines that round the thatch-eves run;
To bend with apples the moss'd cottage trees,
    And fill all fruit with ripeness to the core;
        To swell the gourd, and plump the hazel shells
    With a sweet kernel; to set budding more,
And still more, later flowers for the bees,
Until they think warm days will never cease,
        For Summer has o'er brimmed their clammy cells.

Who hath not seen thee oft amid thy store?
    Sometimes whoever seeks abroad may find
Thee sitting careless on a granary floor,
    Thy hair soft-lifted by the winnowing wind;

Or on a half-reap'd furrow sound asleep,
  Drows'd with the fume of poppies, while thy hook
    Spares the next swath and all its twined flowers:
And sometimes like a gleaner thou dost keep
  Steady thy laden head across a brook;
  Or by a cyder-press, with patient look,
    Thou watchest the last oozings hours by hours.

Where are the songs of Spring? Ay, where are they?
  Think not of them, thou hast thy music too,—
While barred clouds bloom the soft-dying day,
  And touch the stubble-plains with rosy hue;
Then in a wallful choir the small gnats mourn
  Among the river sallows, borne aloft
    Or sinking as the light wind lives or dies;
And full-grown lambs loud bleat from hilly bourn;
  Hedge-crickets sing; and now with treble soft
The red-breast whistles from a garden-croft;
    And gathering swallows twitter in the skies.

Remembrance of Things Past

Allow me to tip my hat—to the Western literary canon, the English curriculum everywhere, and my own distant past— for what is the first and only time in this whole series of Ten Poems. As is surely the case for countless other individuals over the last two hundred years, this magnificent ode by John Keats has managed to survive somewhere in the recesses of my brain for the whole of my adult life.

It was the first poem I ever learned by heart, the first poem I was warmed by, the first poem I heard a teacher treat as something more than an academic exercise. You probably have your own classic poem that lives in you in its own way. As I said in the introduction, a poem does not need to have stood the test of time to be able to accompany you down through the years. Even so, a poem like this one, that has weathered changing tastes and styles over a couple of centuries, clearly strikes a universal chord that transcends time and place (though perhaps you may need to shake away the associations of high school and English exams in order to feel that resonance).

For me, however, my associations of that time have served only to heighten my appreciation for what I learned then. In those couple of years, from sixteen to eighteen, my imagination awoke from what seemed like a slumber. I fell into the unusual situation of being in a class of just three students, and each of my three teachers, for English, French, and history, were in love with their subjects and communicated that love to us.

I grew up in a fold of the Cotswold hills on the edge of the city of Bath, in England, an environment particularly conducive to a romantic turn of mind. Nature had been like a second mother to me throughout my growing years, but it was only when I began to read Keats, as well as Wordsworth's "Prelude," that I found my own unconscious associations brought into the light of day through language.

And what language! The ode "To Autumn" does not seem to me to carry any deeper message than its literal meaning. It does not—in my mind, at least—set off echoes of deep philosophical or even especially existential ruminations, other than that all things shall pass in the course of time. No, what keeps it fresh in me is first and foremost the sensuous, clear-seeing, sense-awakening language, constructed in such a way as to offer a lyric hymn to nature that has no equal anywhere.

> *Season of mists and mellow fruitfulness,*
> *Close bosom-friend of the maturing sun;*

Say what you like, these lines are immortal lines, and their beauty, I am willing to wager, will always resist analysis, whichever school of literary criticism you may wish to apply to them. New criticism, modernist, post-modernist, deconstructionist, they will argue forever about Keats's influences, his intentions, his politics, his contribution to the Romantic cause. Meanwhile, people mutter those lines to themselves over and again, as if taken up in some poetic trance.

And that is exactly what these lines do. They enchant. The lines of this poem are literally stunning. They stun the ordinary mind. They put it on hold and, as if we were on some hypnotist's couch, they lead us into a world of their own which, of course, we recognize as a country that lives in us, too. And Keats weaves this spell with sound, rhyme, lilt, and sway, all the old shaman's tricks of the trade. No wonder the first poetry was sung to the gods. The Greek ode was sung so that the singer and his company could be transported out of themselves and become one with the god. Keats knew what he was doing when he called this an ode. His odes—all written in the year 1819, just two years before his death in Rome of tuberculosis at the age of twenty-six—are considered to be among his greatest works.

So why does that first line stick so fast in the mind? Mmm, the alliteration, those *m*'s, help, of course. The letter *m* is a bountiful letter—think mother, ma, more, much, most, many, M&M's. It's a soft letter, too, made with the lips alone. Then the rhythm carries us along, as it does through the whole poem. And the words themselves are moist and luscious—*mists, mellow,* and *fruitfulness.* The kind of words that whet the taste buds, the kind you may like to savor and roll around on your tongue. A sensuous string of words; a love of the feminine, of fertility, seeps all around them, and spills over to the next line, with its specific reference to *bosom*, and its idea of the season, autumn, nestling up to the *maturing* (father) *sun.*

It's a sense-laden, sexy beginning, and it doesn't stop there. She (autumn) conspires with the sun to fructify the world, and this first stanza amounts to a song in praise of all the results (the offspring) they might expect. Keats paints a picture groaning with abundance and plenty, but in such a way as to make your mouth water with the promise of it all; all swelling and plumping, budding and *o'er brimmed,* and *clammy* to boot.

In my case, a vein of nostalgia only adds to the brew, as it did for the Romantics themselves. The past was entwined for them with an indefinable longing, for . . . for what? It was the feeling itself that mattered to them, more than the specifics it was attached to. The *thatch-eves, the moss'd cottage trees, the hazel shells* are all elements of the image that memory has concocted from the time and place of my adolescence. There are other, darker elements to the real picture, certainly—the narrow-mindedness of the local villagers, my family's outsider status, coming as we did from London when I was seven; our difficult financial circumstances—but memory is selective, and my images from that time dwell far more on the succor and consolation that nature gave me. How bountiful life is, despite all its hardships. What beauty surrounds us, if only we care to look up and notice. This, in my later teens, is what Keats and Wordsworth gave voice to for me. Read the first stanza of this ode and remain sober if you can!

The second stanza personifies autumn the way a classical painting might an old Greek urn. Or imagine one of the painter Rossetti's women (Dante Gabriel Rossetti was born just a few years after Keats's death): thick, flowing, auburn tresses; large, melancholy eyes; pale, strong, sensuous face. Lying, languid, on a granary floor

> *Or on a half-reap'd furrow sound asleep,*
> *Drows'd with the fume of poppies, . . .*

This, I think, is exactly what Keats intends the effect of his poem to be on us. His images seduce. He bathes us in strong, heady odors, in *oozings*, not to make us unconscious, but to lead us into a dimension in which we can feel the stroke of autumn on our skin and on our tongue. The full-bodied, sensuous experience of this season, as painted by Keats, makes the figure of her personification not only attractive but desirable.

And then in the final stanza he pulls us back out of the spell, back to the wonderings and questioning of the reflective faculty.

> *Where are the songs of Spring? Ay, where are they?*
> *Think not of them, thou hast thy music too,*

Autumn, the falling away of all things, has its own beauty, all golds, deep reds, and yellows. Keats, at the age of twenty-four, is not fooled by the apparent eternity and delights of youth. Maturity, and the onset of age, have their own blessings, and in this poem, Keats inspires us to savor them. There is a majesty to the setting sun, *the soft-dying day.* There is a grace, even as there is a sadness, in letting go what comes. There is a beauty in the song of the English robin, the redbreast, the bird of approaching winter, and in the twittering of the departing swallows.

In this last stanza, Keats reminds me once more of a painting, a specific one this time. It is the self-portrait that Rembrandt painted in 1658, when he had just lost both his wife and his fortune. He was fifty-two years old. It is in the Frick Museum in New York City. Rembrandt portrays himself in a rich smock of deep gold. His back is straight, his solemn face looms out of the shadows. His eyes gaze out of the painting and engage whomever is looking. This is who I am, they say. I have come to this pass in my life, and I am not afraid. The essential dignity of being human shines out of those eyes, out beyond all his losses. They are eyes of compassion and wisdom; they are the eyes of a man of years. This monumental achievement of John Keats, his ode "To Autumn," is a reminder, among all its other qualities, of the truth and the beauty that can come only with time.

9

THE ART OF DISAPPEARING

by Naomi Shihab Nye

When they say Don't I know you?
say no.

When they invite you to the party
remember what parties are like
before answering.

Someone telling you in a loud voice
they once wrote a poem.
Greasy sausage balls on a paper plate.
Then reply.

If they say We should get together
say Why?

It's not that you don't love them anymore.
You're trying to remember something
too important to forget.

Trees. The monastery bell at twilight.
Tell them you have a new project.
It will never be finished.

When someone recognizes you in a grocery store
nod briefly and become a cabbage.
When someone you haven't seen in ten years
appears at the door,
don't start singing him all your new songs.
You will never catch up.

Walk around feeling like a leaf.
Know you could tumble any second.
Then decide what to do with your time.

You Could Tumble Any Second

I find the strong and sober stand of this poem a welcome in-
spiration. Yet I know there are those who feel otherwise.
People have told me they feel it to be ungenerous and cur-
mudgeonly in its attitude to others. On the other hand, I re-
member seeing Bill Moyers on PBS one evening, and him
saying that ever since being called into the hospital for heart
trouble, he has kept a copy of this poem by Naomi Shihab
Nye in his top pocket. For me, it's that kind of poem. A re-
minder poem, a shake-your-tree poem, a wake-up-and-live-
your-own-life-before-it's-all-too-late poem.

Most of us need help with prioritizing, with living by our
deepest needs instead of according to the dictates of social
custom and other people's expectations. And this poem is
one of those that comes running to help, if we are willing to
sit down with its lines and read them out loud to ourselves as
if they were a message from a trusted friend. Which they are.
The friend is the persistent murmur in our own chest, which
Nye has heard and, I believe, correctly translated. The same
murmur must have arisen in her own early mornings. Any
true sound of our own will always have an echo in other

hearts. It was Keats, after all, who said, in a letter to John Taylor in 1818, that

> Poetry should strike the reader as a wording of his own highest thoughts, and appear almost as a Remembrance.

The note struck by this poem will not echo in everyone, of course. It may be that the truest thing for you to do is precisely to go to as many parties as you can. Perhaps you have lived too long alone. Perhaps greasy sausage balls on a paper plate are a welcome relief from too many meals eaten on your own while standing in front of the refrigerator door. What may matter for you, and far more than the quality of the food, may be the animal warmth of human contact, the return to the human fold, a sense of belonging in even the most mundane of conversations, the most ordinary of company. There is a place for gossip, lame jokes, and small talk. They can serve as a temporary glue to bind us back into the world of others.

But that is not the position Nye is taking in this poem. There may be a time for small talk, but for Nye, that time is not now. She is fierce here in her need to forgo small comforts. Nye doesn't mince words. She suggests our need for social contact is hiding a deeper need, perhaps as yet not fully conscious. The one she really wants to come home to in this poem is herself. And that is not often easy in the twitter and chatter of casual exchanges. She is talking to herself here.

Telling herself to resist the temptations of the social network. Her poem reminds me of one by Rumi, in which he says that it's already late, it's starting to rain, and he wants to go home.

> *We've wandered long enough in empty buildings.*
> *I know it's tempting to stay and meet those new people.*[1]

But, he says, he wants to go home. Naomi Shihab Nye, too, remembers what parties are *actually* like, rather than fantasizing about an *idea* of them, a picture perhaps of warmth, friendship, and meaningful conversation. The reality: junk food and loud voices wanting you to listen.

Like you, perhaps, I have sometimes opted for the idea of what some event might be rather than what I know from experience is likely to be the reality. While it is true that I do like to mingle, to feel I am in the thick of it all, the pleasure is usually fleeting. It is often not long before I start to feel I am skating on surfaces, especially my own. By the end of the party—no, well before the end—I am thinking of my studio with its view over a garden, and the long evenings of quiet I enjoy there.

It's not that the figure in this poem is a misanthrope, a social misfit, or a hapless introvert.

> *It's not that you don't love them anymore.*

This is an important line. Many of us, especially women, find it difficult to do what we long in our hearts to do because of a fear of hurting others. Because they might think we don't appreciate them, love them anymore. Especially if what you need is solitude; if

> *You're trying to remember something*
> *too important to forget.*
> *Trees. The monastery bell at twilight.*

Trees—presences that sway in the wind through all our depressions and elations. Still there, joining sky to earth, wherever we are in our mood cycles. Monastery bells, the sound that has tolled for millennia, reminding the generations of another life, another way, a deeper note that longs, even now, to be struck in the human heart.

This is the note that Naomi Shihab Nye has heard. This is why she has more urgent things on her mind than small talk. There comes a time when you have to decide what kind of life you are going to live. Will you live by the dictates of your social persona, or by the softer, more genuine voice that you hear sometimes at twilight, or before falling asleep? Both have a place, but there are times when the latter must be followed, whatever the cost, if something precious in you is not to die.

When you know this from the inside out, there will be no need to impress others with your stories. When someone you haven't seen for ten years appears at the door, you won't need to

> *. . . start singing him all your new songs.*

Someone very dear to me died recently. His name was Ray Gatchalian.[2] No one who knew him ever expected to see him die. He seemed immortal. A green beret in Vietnam, fire captain for the Oakland Fire Department, rescuer of street kids in Mongolia, filmmaker, peace activist extraordinaire, poet. His death was mourned across the country, and in some of the more far-flung corners of the world. We put a large photo of Ray on our coffee table, so anyone coming into our house could see him. When people arrived, we would tell them one of his incredible stories. Our friends were politely respectful, but we could see they hadn't really caught the magic of who Ray was. Then they saw the photograph. They saw his glorious smile. They saw his generous eyes. And they knew. We didn't need to say anything else. Ray wasn't his stories. He was the light in his eyes.

Ray died on a remote road in Chile. His car had flipped over around a bend. He had got out and hitched a ride from the next vehicle, which happened to be a garbage truck. Ray climbed in, the driver drove off, and a few minutes later plunged hundreds of feet into a ravine. They were found two days later.

Who would have thought it? Ray, of all people. Ray, who poured all of his abundant energy into caring for others, dying unknown to anyone on a distant hillside. Death comes when and how it wants to. It's not personal. Not a statement or an indictment about what you have or haven't done. It will come to your best friend, of all people. None of us is immune to that tap on the shoulder. None of us knows when or where that tap will come. It's been said so often, but do we ever really hear it?

I wonder what our lives would feel like if we lived with the knowing that soon, any time, everything we treasured and worried ourselves over would be brushed to one side like the nonchalant flourish of a magician's cloak? For most of us, death is a concept; something that happens to others, but not to us. Not to the person we share our lives with. Not to our own children. Except that it does, and sometimes, far sooner than we think. Ray's death brought this home to me in a way that not even the death of my parents had done. His death reminded me of the wisdom in Nye's final lines:

> *Walk around feeling like a leaf.*
> *Know you could tumble at any second.*
> Then *decide what to do with your time.*

This is the deep spirit that runs through this poem. Far from being ungenerous, I believe it calls us to what really matters most in our lives: to that in us which is truly alive.

> *I praise what is truly alive,*

said Goethe, in his poem, "The Holy Longing." [3] "The Art of Disappearing," in its own way, calls us to this kind of praising.

10

THE MIND OF ABSOLUTE TRUST

by Seng-Ts'an   *(Excerpt)*

The Great Way isn't difficult
* for those who are unattached to their preferences.*
Let go of longing and aversion,
* and everything will be perfectly clear.*
When you cling to a hairbreadth of distinction,
* heaven and earth are set apart.*
If you want to realize the truth,
* don't be for or against.*
The struggle between good and evil
* is the primal disease of the mind.*
Not grasping the deeper meaning,
* you just trouble your mind's serenity.*
As vast as infinite space,
* it is perfect and lacks nothing.*
But because you select and reject,
* you can't perceive its true nature.*

Don't get entangled in the world;
   don't lose yourself in emptiness.
Be at peace in the oneness of things,
   and all errors will disappear by themselves.

If you don't live in the Tao,
   you fall into assertion or denial.
Asserting that the world is real,
   you are blind to its deeper reality;
denying that the world is real,
   you are blind to the selflessness of all things.
The more you think about these matters,
   the farther you are from the truth.
Step aside from all thinking,
   and there is nowhere you can't go.
Returning to the root, you find the meaning;
   chasing appearances, you lose their source.
At the moment of profound insight,
   you transcend both appearance and emptiness.
Don't keep searching for the truth;
   just let go of your opinions.

—TRANSLATED BY STEPHEN MITCHELL

It's That Simple!

Ah, if only it were that simple! But if it *seems* so difficult, does that make it any the less true? True that

> *The Great Way isn't difficult*
> *for those who are unattached to their preferences.*

In reality, to be unattached to one's preferences is both the easiest thing in the world and apparently one of the most difficult. Difficult, because all too often, our preferences are who we think we are. When we feel a preference intensely, it's as if it defines us an individual. It seems to be what we *need*, rather than what we want; and without its satisfaction, it can even seem as if we might cease to exist. Think of a three-year-old child, arm outstretched, wailing, whose very life seems to depend on having that ice cream. Sometimes, we are not that different.

And yet one of the greatest Buddhist teachers of all time, Seng-Ts'an, the third Chinese patriarch, assures us in this inspired wisdom poem—a poem that has served as instruction for Buddhists for fifteen hundred years—that it is nowhere near as difficult as we might think. Perhaps it requires only the smallest shift of perspective. A shift in our sense of who we are that allows us to see in another light whether getting what we want is, after all, a matter of life and death.

Seng-Ts'an is not, you may have noticed, urging us to turn our back on things, on people, or places. It is not the things of this world that separate us from what he calls the Great Way. How different this is to the teachings of the dualistic traditions of the West; and especially perhaps Christianity, which, out of fear, has always endowed the world, and in particular women, with the tempting power of the devil.

Nor are preferences themselves an obstruction as far as Seng-Ts'an is concerned. To have preferences is entirely natural. They come with the human package. They are part of the starter kit. Seng-Ts'an isn't telling us not to have preferences. That would be like telling us not to have thoughts. Rather, he is saying that if you loosen your *attachment* to a preference, then that, in itself, already opens up a larger space in consciousness. With a spacious consciousness, the Great Way opens up.

The Great Way was also known in China as the Tao. The way things are. The natural course of things, left to its own intelligent design, like any great river or the smallest stream.

The Tao
> *pours out everything into life—*
It is a cornucopia
>> *that never runs dry.*

It is the deep source of everything—
　　　　it is nothing, and yet in everything.[1]

This is how the *Tao Te Ching* describes it. The *Tao Te Ching*, attributed to the Taoist master Lao Tse, was first written down in the first century B.C., some four hundred years after Lao Tse's death. Taoism, a way without a way, so to speak—without a codified dogma or teaching—pointed instead to a manner of being in the world. And this poem by Seng-Ts'an gives eloquent voice to that way of being.

"The Mind of Absolute Trust," as the poem came to be called in English, is the earliest known fusion of the teachings of Mahayana Buddhism and Taoism.[2] Buddhism first came over the mountains to China from India in the person of Bodhidharma, around 530 A.D. Bodhidharma's teachings found fertile ground in Taoist China, and the great master soon became known as the first patriarch of Buddhism there. Seng-Ts'an, a layman, came to the second patriarch, Hui-k'o, with a request for the master's teachings. The story goes that Seng-Ts'an was a leper, and that when the patriarch implied that he could not teach someone in such a hazardous state of health, the layman replied, "Even if my body is sick, the heart-mind of a sick person is no different from your heart-mind." Hui-k'o immediately realized the spiritual capacity of the leper, accepted him as a student, and later confirmed him as his successor, the third patriarch.

What is wonderful about this wisdom poem is that you

don't have to be a Buddhist, a Taoist, or anything else, to in-
tuit the truth of it. Its wisdom is universal.

Let go of longing and aversion,
and everything will be perfectly clear.

No formal instruction is obligatory, no memorization of
texts, no donning of robes, no adherence to any dogma or
code. This teaching is direct and experiential. Its efficacy de-
pends not on tradition, or received authority, but on your
willingness to see directly into your own mind. Into the dy-
namics of attraction and repulsion, the way they imprison
our attention, our very life energy, and keep us captive in a
world of duality, and therefore in suffering. This kind of see-
ing takes work, in the sense of a commitment; but the more
you see, the more you will want to see.

The Englishman J. G. Bennett, an inveterate seeker after
truth who died in 1975 of a heart attack while instructing
pupils in the Gurdjieff system of movements, once went to
India to visit a renowned sage, Shivapuri Baba.[3] The baba,
who was reputed to be around 137 years old at the time, had
lived for 40 years in solitude in the forest, and had then
made a decades-long pilgrimage on foot around the world.
On the way, he met Queen Victoria and the American
president, among many other Western dignitaries. When
Bennett met him, he was living in a remote hermitage in the
Himalayas, far removed from the guru circuits popular
among Westerners at the time. Bennett asked him what he
considered to be the most essential teaching he could offer.

"Strive to be free of likes and dislikes," Shivapuri Baba replied. "If you cannot do that, you might as well take up a religion."

If, even for a moment, this moment, we are able to set aside the struggle, to

Let go of longing and aversion,

the muddy waters of the mind will settle and what will be left is the way things are. Our mind, in its simplicity and clarity, will reflect the natural order of things and what is wanting to happen of its own accord. What is wanting to happen, that is, according to the movement of our own unconscious as well as of the tide of the collective life of which we are a part.

> *If you want to realize the truth,*
> *don't be for or against.*
> *The struggle between good and evil*
> *is the primal disease of the mind.*

These few lines are a profound challenge for us as Westerners. Two thousand years of schooling in right and wrong, good and bad, encourage us to think in moral and ethical terms rather than from the perspective of spiritual philosophy. Not only that, but the human brain is hard wired to perceive the world dualistically. The oriental mind is different from ours, not in its hard wiring, but in its acculturation. For thousands of years, the cultures of India and China, especially, have lived in a world view in which the Dark and the Light arise from the same Source. Though there is a continual dance, struggle, or dialectic between these two forces, they are always fundamentally part of an undivided Whole. In the great Indian epic, the Ramayana, the arch-devil, Ravana, is in fact a great spiritual being who is more devoted to Ram, the personification of the Light, than anyone. Their struggle was his way of getting close to Ram and being touched by Him. So who, then, from this perspective, is Saddam Hussein, or Osama bin Laden, or George Bush? We are so quick to know what is right and wrong. There is undoubtedly an ethical level of reality from which we can judge acts to be, in the West we would say, good or evil. Yet the Taoists and the Buddhists would consider this to be a relative level of reality. In Buddhism, they would use the terms *dharma* and *adharma,* which, with a little license, means "with the way, or against the way of things."

Our Western terms carry a heavy value judgment; the Buddhist terms are more neutral, pointing instead to a scheme of life that includes, but goes beyond the moral ground. At root, the Oriental perspective points beyond the mind altogether. It implies there is a wisdom, a way of things at work, whose designs we can never really know. Ultimately, it points beyond words altogether, to a condition of Don't Know Mind.

It's not that the forces of light and dark do not exist; of course they do, as we can see just by looking around us. But,

> *Not grasping the deeper meaning,*
> *you just trouble your mind's serenity.*

Or, as the Sufi poet and sage Hafiz said,

> *. . . There are plays within plays that you*
> *cannot see.*[4]

Then Rumi:

> *Out beyond ideas of wrongdoing and rightdoing,*
> *there is a field. I'll meet you there.*[5]

Mystics of the world—those who have fallen into the current that gave rise to all religions and all things, the current the ancient Chinese called the Tao—are united on this: that there is an intelligence to life and all its struggles that is deeper than the moral ground, even though that moral ground has profound value on its own terms. There is always a larger picture that we cannot see, objectify, or quite put into words; a bigger view that we can intuit by living in the more spacious mind that we walk into by means of the door of not knowing.

Not knowing does not signify dullness, or having no interest or curiosity. On the contrary, I would imagine it to be a condition of unusual aliveness; a condition in which we are not outside the stream of events, looking in, but inside the stream, part of it, while aware of it all at the same time. As if our own small breath became joined to the big breath of the world—which it always is, of course, except now we know it to be so; not as a piece of information, but as a movement of the blood.

Don't get entangled in the world;

Does this mean we don't act? That we don't take up the struggle on behalf of something we know to be justified, because we can intuit a bigger picture whose deeper wisdom lies hidden? I don't think so. Far from a philosophy of noninvolvement, I think Seng-Ts'an's poem encourages a full immersion into life, whatever that might signify for us personally. If it is our "way," our destiny we might say, to heal the sufferings of the world in whatever form is meaningful to us, then we will do that, even as we know that there will always be suffering on earth; and that the roots of suffering lie far beneath our understanding. If it is our "way" to take up arms in the defense of everything we hold dear, then we shall do so, just "because."

It is not, after all, that we should opt for the world of spaciousness and clarity over the relative, chaotic experience of daily existence:

don't lose yourself in emptiness

the poet goes on to say. It is neither this world nor the next that bars our way. It is our attachment to our concepts that confuses the mind. It is our tendency to reify the ineffable that reduces it to another code to beat someone else over the head with. Spiritual is no better than worldly; it is different, and not so different as you might think. In this way of seeing, the Taoist way, to name something is to beat it over a head with a club and deliver it as a trophy.

It goes on and on, the sublime wisdom of this poem. I can

only stand like a fool before it and burp out responses. It coaxes the gasbag out of me, and makes me a living example of how not to live it. Write about it instead. So I will, though not for much longer. What else can I do?

Look at these lines:

> *Asserting that the world is real,*
> *   you are blind to its deeper reality;*
> *denying that the world is real,*
> *   you are blind to the selflessness of all things.*

A perfect occasion for me to trot out my favorite Hindu saying:

> *The world is unreal.*
> *Brahman alone is real.*
> *Brahman is the world.*[6]

Oh God, Brahman, Zeus, all of you, come to my aid! These few words have me rolling on the floor every time, flailing like a minnow in the jaws of this mind-snapping paradox. It's both, every time, isn't it? Or on the other hand, neither this nor that. Now I know why some of the Zen schools have always loved paradox in the form of a koan or impossible question. It just cracks you open. That's what Seng-Ts'an's words do. They crack you open.

> *The more you think about these matters,*
> *   the farther you are from the truth.*

Okay . . . so that's why he says finally, in the last lines of this excerpt (which is about half of the full text)

Don't keep searching for the truth;
just let go of your opinions.

Doesn't that knock you off your perch? It does me. All the meaningful and deeply serious questing after the meaning of life, in whatever way may be attractive to you, is ultimately unnecessary. Even the idea that there is anything to look for is a misunderstanding. Not that we don't bother; that we just forget about it all and get on with the business of earning our first million. No, it's neither this nor that; all he is asking us to do is to undertake the small work of freeing our attachment to our opinions. If we do that, it really doesn't matter what else we do.

So you see, the Don't Know Mind is mind-boggling. Seng-Ts'an's verses are mind-stopping. The only way I can think of to end this rant is to borrow the words of T. S. Eliot:

The only wisdom we can hope to acquire
Is the wisdom of humility: humility is endless.[7]

11

WHEN DEATH COMES

by Mary Oliver

When death comes
like the hungry bear in autumn;
when death comes and takes all the bright coins from his purse

to buy me, and snaps the purse shut;
when death comes
like the measle-pox;

when death comes
like an iceberg between the shoulder blades,

I want to step through the door full of curiosity, wondering:
what is it going to be like, that cottage of darkness?

And therefore I look upon everything
as a brotherhood and a sisterhood,
and I look upon time as no more than an idea,
and I consider eternity as another possibility,

and I think of each life as a flower, as common
as a field daisy, and as singular,

and each name a comfortable music in the mouth,
tending, as all music does, toward silence,

and each body a lion of courage, and something
precious to the earth.

When it's over, I want to say: all my life
I was a bride married to amazement.
I was the bridegroom, taking the world into my arms.

When it's over, I don't want to wonder
if I have made of my life something particular, and real.
I don't want to find myself sighing and frightened,
or full of argument.

I don't want to end up simply having visited this world.

Amazing

There is a poem by Mary Oliver in each one of the Ten Poems books, and though there are ten thousand poets to choose from every time, here I am again, choosing one of her beautiful poems—as finely cut and polished as a gemstone—to end this, the final book in the series. How could I write a book called *Ten Poems to Last a Lifetime*, and, knowing this poem of hers, "When Death Comes," not include it as one of the ten? Easily, you might say: Just read a few more anthologies, gather more material. But why, when this poem raises the hair on my forearm with every reading? When I know I shall be muttering these lines for years to come, as I have done already for a decade or more?

Like you, perhaps, I have wondered at times how death will come to me. But never, in my wonderings, have images like these flown across my horizon, like the ones Oliver begins this poem with.

> *When death comes*
> *like the hungry bear in autumn;*

I can see him now, that bulky black creature, all hunched over, loping full of intent toward the honey jar of my body, his strong paws raised ready to break me open. There is no discussion with such a ravenous creature; his gait has a finality that is reserved for only this, our last act.

And then the *purse* and the *bright coins*. Whatever the price tag around your neck, death can pay. No one is too expensive for him. There is nothing and no one his money can't buy. But what really drives this image home for me is the purse snapping shut. Again, the deliberate finality. Oliver sharpens our ears and our eyes in this image, then, in the next one,

> *when death comes*
> *like the measle-pox;*

has our flesh crawling. Doesn't the pox break out all over, and, unlike the bear or a decisive purchase, take hold of us gradually, one piece at a time? Her final image of death is for me the most sinister, the most original, of all:

> *when death comes*
> *like an iceberg between the shoulder blades,*

For it can hit us from behind, when we are looking the other way, when we least expect it. And death is cold, implacable as an iceberg, relentless and unremitting in its blow at our backbone. If it can sink the *Titanic*, what chance do *we* stand? Not only do the images crowd in one upon the other like a gathering storm, but the repetition of the phrase *when death comes . . . when death comes . . .* adds to the mounting lyrical intensity.

And what is Oliver building up to, but a couple of lines that release all the expectancy and free our breath and attention the way an open door offers the possibility of a wider horizon:

> *I want to step through the door full of curiosity, wondering:*
> *what is it going to be like, that cottage of darkness?*

She takes us up to the very edge, to the threshold of death, and then, in her imagination, lifts her foot to step right on through. Can you feel how these lines bring a bigger breath to your lungs? How, suddenly, all the menace, all the fear of death, is gone, and in its place is a childlike excitement, the kind of anticipation one feels when landing in a country one has never been to before? Mary Oliver's work is full of curiosity; nature in all its forms delights and amazes her, as does the wonder of life itself. Now she tells us she wants to carry that same wonderment through death's door; for surely, isn't whatever happens next—if anything—the greatest source of curiosity and debate that human beings have known since time began?

All the theories and speculations are of no interest to her, though. She is curious precisely because she doesn't know. Here, as elsewhere in her work, Oliver maintains a precious innocence in response to what is before her. This is why, so often, she is able to see with eyes that are fresh as a child's.

It is only in the open state of not knowing that genuine curiosity can arise, and such a condition, far from being naïve, is the mark of the wise.

And yet there is one phrase—*that cottage of darkness*—that suggests the feeling state that she brings to the anticipation of death. That the afterlife is for us, the living, an unknown territory, and therefore a darkness, is an assumption we would expect. But a *cottage?* Mary Oliver, far from being afraid of death, appears to respond to it as she would to home. A cottage is a homey place, a place of safety and warmth. She is going home, even if the lights are out and she cannot see who or what is there to welcome her.

And what is the value of stepping up to death's door in this poem, and wondering what it holds for her? Surely it is the outlook, the attitude it fosters while she is still here, on the living side. Because she has touched the hem of death, the reality of it, and *because she was not afraid,* Oliver cannot help but see life differently.

> *And therefore I look upon everything*
> *as a brotherhood and a sisterhood,*

These lines and the several that follow them are full not just of curiosity, but of love. She realizes her natural kinship with all and everything, how everything that lives and breathes is gathered in a unity invisible to our normal eyes. And if time is *no more than an idea,* then the threads that connect join us to everyone and everything that ever lived, and that shall ever live. "As it was in the beginning, now, and ever shall be."

Let your heart rest, for a moment, on the loving, compassionate regard of these few lines:

> *and I think of each life as a flower, as common*
> *as a field daisy, and as singular,*
>
> *and each name a comfortable music in the mouth,*
> *tending, as all music does, toward silence,*
>
> *and each body a lion of courage, and something*
> *precious to the earth.*

Your life, and mine, as common and unique as a single daisy among a field of daisies. And your mother's life, too; your ex-husband's, the neighbor's, the one you haven't spoken to for years. No one, nothing, left out.

> *For you are only one thing among many.*
> *And whoever sees that way heals his heart,[1]*

says Czeslaw Milosz, in his poem "Love." This is the way Mary Oliver sees in her poem, although she adds that our commonality does nothing to diminish our particularity. Whoever we are, our name, the mark of our individuality, tastes and sounds to her ears like music, and every name leads in the end to the mystery, to silence. And our bodies, whether broken, whole, ugly, or beautiful, every body is courageous simply for the fact of being here, knowing it will be broken in the end on time's wheel. How precious this human body is! No wonder the Buddhists sing its praises so, assuring us that beings wait for thousands of incarnations for the grace and the gift of a body like ours.

This is the way Mary Oliver wants to live:

> *When it's over, I want to say: all my life*
> *I was a bride married to amazement.*
> *I was the bridegroom, taking the world into my arms.*

A bride married to amazement: Is this not a string of words to bring tears to your eyes? Imagine living your life this way, heart and eyes open wide to the world, so much in love with the life you are given to live that you feel joined to it by holy sacrament, the sacrament of love. This marriage, the one with your life, is indeed until death do you part, no second chances.

And this is the way Mary Oliver doesn't want to live:

> *When it's over, I don't want to wonder*
> *if I have made of my life something particular, and real.*
> *I don't want to find myself sighing and frightened,*
> *or full of argument.*

How many of us live out our days in regret, in bitterness, or disappointment, as if our lot were unfair? How many of us end up talking about all the things we would have liked to do, and be, and didn't, and weren't? There is no excuse, really, however harsh it may sound. We can live the life we have because our life is in our hands, not in anyone else's.

> *One day you finally knew*
> *what you had to do, and began,*[2]

Oliver says in her poem "The Journey." And this is the way that same poem ends:

> *determined to save*
> *the only life you could save.*

Mary Oliver, in all of her poems, is the most passionate advocate of full immersion. She urges our utmost participation in the life that opens up before us daily—not a social participation, or a cultural one (these are not her subjects), but a direct immersion into the moment we are presented with. Falling into life is precisely what allows us to see everyone and everything as a brother or a sister. It is the simplest, deepest expression of love; and of a communion that ennobles, rather than diminishes, our individuality.

> *I don't want to end up simply having visited this world.*

she cries, finally, a cry from the heart. For this is the antithesis of love, to be isolated in one's sense of separateness (as this line is isolated in space); to let life pass us by without being touched by it. This, for Oliver, is the greatest tragedy, and she is shaking herself, and us, awake; alerting us to the way we can so easily let the world slip through our fingers. Let us end with two lines from her poem "The Summer Day," which say it this way:

> *Tell me, what is it you plan to do*
> *with your one wild and precious life?*[3]

Epilogue

This, then, will be the last book in the Ten Poems series. My hope is that you will continue to discover in poetry the inspiration to make the changes you need in your life—to open your heart to the big sky of the world, to free yourself from the weight of tired attitudes and ideas—inspiration, in short, that will last you a lifetime. And if I have a wish, it is that you have had as much enjoyment and nourishment in reading one or more of these books as I've had in writing them.

I encourage you to seek out fresh sources of your own, to continue, as ever, reading poetry aloud to yourself or to a friend; to memorize your favorite poems, and even to take the leap of writing some lines of your own. After all, why not? Poetry has been with us since time began, and has been kept alive through the centuries by countless individuals who, without any thought for posterity, sang out or wrote down what they saw in their mind's eye, what they felt in their grieving or loving heart. For guidance in writing, look to Mary Oliver's *A Poetry Handbook,* or her *Rules for the Dance: A Handbook for Writing and Reading Metrical Verse,* and read Dorianne Laux's *The Poet's Companion: A Guide to the Pleasures of Writing Poetry*. And above all, as Fleur Adcock said so succinctly in that interview for the *Guardian,* "It's about words. You hear them, read them, then you write. But mostly read. Read the bloody poems."

Poetry, of course, is just one of the many portals that a new way of seeing, a new life, even, can use to announce itself, to step from the shadows into our lived experience. The sight of a cloud in a blue sky is another way; or those tree roots twisting around each other like so many fingers; a paper bag bobbing in a sudden wind. Painting is another window onto a life lived in a larger way; sculpture and music, too. What matters in the end is not so much the medium as the message. Does it enliven us, awaken us, move us forward in our lives? Or does it dampen us down and close us off from ourselves and the living world? Poetry and all the arts serve us most when they nourish the soul, the spirit, rather than sophistry, cynicism, and bitterness. The best poetry is indeed the song, the ode, of the human soul, and it is this song that the present series has attempted to sing.

About the Poets

BILLY COLLINS (b.1941) is professor of English at Lehman College, the City University of New York. He lives in Somers, New York. No poet since Robert Frost has managed to combine high critical acclaim with such popular appeal. The typical Collins poem opens on a clear and hospitable note but soon takes an unexpected turn. Poems that begin in irony may end in a moment of lyrical surprise. No wonder Collins sees his poetry as "a form of travel writing," and considers humor "a door into the serious." The author of seven volumes of poetry, Collins was poet laureate of the United States from 2001 to 2003.

HAYDEN CARRUTH (b.1921) was born in Connecticut and educated at the University of North Carolina at Chapel Hill and the University of Chicago. He has spent much of his life in northern Vermont, though he now lives in upstate New York, where until recently he taught in the graduate creative writing program at Syracuse University. He has published twenty-nine books, mostly poetry, but also four books of criticism and two anthologies. His collection *Scrambled Eggs and Whiskey* won the National

Book Award for Poetry. He has also won the National Book Critics Circle Award, the Lannan Award, and many other honors.

FLEUR ADCOCK (b.1937) was born in New Zealand and moved with her family to England when she was five, remaining there through World War II until 1950, when the family went back to New Zealand. In 1963, after divorcing her first husband, she returned to England permanently with one of her two children, the other son remaining with his father in New Zealand. Until 1980, except for a year when she went to live the life of a recluse in the English Lake District, she was a professional librarian. It was during that year that she wrote the poem in this book. Since 1980 she has been a full-time writer, translator, and editor.

RAINER MARIA RILKE (1875–1926) survived a lonely and unhappy childhood in Prague to publish his first volume of poetry, *Leben und Lieder,* in 1894. In 1896 he left Prague for the University of Munich, and later made his first trip to Italy, and then to Russia. In 1902 in Paris he became friend and secretary to the sculptor Rodin; the next twelve years there saw his greatest poetic activity. In 1919 he moved to Switzerland, where he wrote his last two works, *Sonnets to Orpheus* and *Duino Elegies,* in 1923. He died in Switzerland, of leukemia, in 1926. His reputation has grown enormously since his death, and he is now considered one of the greatest poets of the twentieth century.

DORIANNE LAUX (b.1952) has an Irish, French, and Algonquin heritage, and grew up in Maine. Between the ages of eighteen and thirty she worked as a gas station manager, sanatorium cook, maid, and doughnut holer. A single mother, she took occasional poetry classes at a local junior college, writing poems during shift breaks. In 1983 she moved to Berkeley and began writing in earnest. Supported by scholarships and grants, she returned to school, and graduated in 1988 with a degree in English. Her first book of poems, *Awake,* was nominated for the San Francisco Bay Area Book Critics Award for Poetry. Her third collection, *Smoke,* was published in 2000.

D. H. LAWRENCE (1885–1930) was an acclaimed English novelist, short story writer, essayist, and poet. Although better known as a novelist, his first published works in 1909 were poems, and his poetry, especially his evocations of the natural world, has since had a significant influence on poets on both sides of the Atlantic. A writer with radical views, Lawrence regarded sex, the primitive subconscious, and nature as cures to what he saw to be the evils of modern industrial society. A lifelong sufferer of tuberculosis, he died in France in 1930.

JAMES WRIGHT (1927–1980) was born in Ohio, graduated from Kenyon College in 1952, and studied in Vienna the following year on a Fulbright scholarship. In 1954 he went on to the University of Washington, where he studied with Stanley Kunitz and Theodore Roethke. *The*

Green Wall was published in 1957, and he began to be published in every important journal from *The New Yorker* to the *New Orleans Poetry Review*. In the early sixties, Wright found a kindred spirit in Robert Bly. Both of them were interested in a poetry that suggested there were vast powers that awaited release. Wright won many awards, including the Pulitzer for his *Collected Poems*. He continued to write in a manner that was deliberately vulnerable, an extension of the "confessional" poetry current in the late fifties, yet transcending the merely personal to reach toward eternal and archetypal themes.

JOHN KEATS (1795–1821) was the last of the great English Romantic poets. When he was born, William Blake was already almost forty, Wordsworth and Coleridge were in their middle twenties, Byron was a boy of seven, and Shelley was just three. Keats was also the most humbly born of them all, his father having run the Swan and Hoop livery stables in central London. Keats's first work, *Poems*, was published in 1817, when he was just twenty-two. In the following three years, he produced his entire output in an astonishing outpouring of creative genius. Next to Wordsworth, Keats is the foremost representative of the Romantic revival of interest in nature. He also held the imagination to be the most important organ of perception. One of his best known couplets, from "Ode on a Grecian Urn," affirms his core belief that

"Beauty is truth, truth beauty,"—that is all
Ye know on earth, and all ye need to know.

NAOMI SHIHAB NYE (b.1952) was born of a Palestinian father and an American mother. Her work consistently reveals the poignancy and the paradoxes that emerge from feeling an intimate relationship with two different cultures. Raised in St. Louis, Missouri, she has lived in Jerusalem and now resides with her family in San Antonio, Texas. Her poems and short stories have appeared in reviews and magazines all over the world. Besides her six volumes of poetry, she has also written books for children and edited several anthologies of prose. She first started writing poetry at the age of six. "Somehow, I knew what a poem was. I liked the comfortable, portable shape of poems . . . and especially the way they took you to a deeper, quieter place, almost immediately."

SENG-TS'AN (6th century A.D.) was a Buddhist layman over forty years of age and suffering from leprosy, when, according to legend, he met the second Chinese Zen patriarch, Hui-k'o. Hui-k'o greeted him with these words: "You are suffering from leprosy, what can you want from me?"

Seng-Ts'an is supposed to have replied. "Even if my body is sick, the heart-mind of a sick person is no different from your heart-mind."

Hui-k'o immediately accepted him as his student, and later confirmed him as his successor, the third patriarch. Seng-Ts'an's great legacy to posterity was the poem in this book, known in Chinese as the *Hsin Hsin Ming*.

MARY OLIVER (b.1935) is one of America's most widely read contemporary poets. The critic Alice Ostriker contends that Oliver is "as visionary as Emerson." She won her first poetry prize at the age of twenty-seven, from the Poetry Society of America, for her collection *No Voyage*. She won the Pulitzer Prize in 1984 for her collection of poems *American Primitive*, and she was winner of the 1992 National Book Award for poetry for her *New and Selected Poems*. In an interview for the *Bloomsbury Review* in 1990, she said, "I feel that the function of the poet is to be . . . somehow instructive and opinionated, useful even if only as a devil's advocate. . . . The question asked today is: 'What does it mean?' Nobody says, 'How does it feel?' "

Notes

INTRODUCTION

1. In the summer of 1960, Jane Goodall arrived on the shore of Lake Tanganyika in East Africa to study the area's chimpanzee population. In 1965, she earned her Ph.D. in ethology at Cambridge and then returned to Tanzania to continue research. Her work over the last thirty-five years has radically changed and enriched the field of primatology. Among her books are *The Chimpanzees I Love: Saving Their World and Ours* (New York: Scholastic, 2001) and *Beyond Innocence: An Autobiography in Letters, The Later Years* (New York: Houghton Mifflin, 2001).

2. Robert Frost (1874–1963) was the great New England poet of the twentieth century. In 1912, at thirty-eight, he moved with his wife and four children to England for three years. Some of his finest poetry was written there, though its inspiration was the people and land of New England. After 1915, he spent the rest of his life on various New England farms as the poet-farmer.

1   MY LIFE

1. Wallace Stevens (1879–1955) said this in an interview, in response to a comment that his poems were obscure. He also said that poetry was his way of making the world palatable. "It's the way of making one's experience, almost wholly inexplicable, explicable." Stevens largely ignored the literary world, and didn't receive wide recognition until the publication of his *Collected Poems*, in 1954, a year before his death. He worked his whole life as an insurance agent and wrote poetry wherever and whenever it came to him.

2. Excerpt from "Forgetfulness" by Billy Collins. In *Sailing Alone Around the Room*. New York: Random House, 2001.

3. Excerpt from "Love" by Czeslaw Milosz. In *New and Collected Poems 1931–2001*. New York: Ecco Press, 2001.

4. Excerpt from "The Layers" by Stanley Kunitz. In *Passing Through: The Later Poems, New and Selected*. New York: Norton, 1995.

2   ECSTASY

1. *Scrambled Eggs and Whiskey: Poems, 1991–1995* by Hayden Carruth. Port Townsend, Wash.: Copper Canyon Press, 1996.

2. *Doctor Jazz: Poems, 1996–2000*. Port Townsend, Wash.: Copper Canyon Press, 2001.

3. For the crucial role played by seventeenth-century England in the development of individualism, see *The Creation of the Modern World: The Untold Story of the British*

Enlightenment by Roy Porter. New York: W. W. Norton, 2001.

4. See *A Brief History of Everything* by Ken Wilber. Boston: Shambhala Publications, 2001.

5. The most celebrated qawwali singer of them all is Nusrat Fateh Ali Khan, from Pakistan. His music is on the Sony label.

6. In 1940, four teenagers discovered the now world-famous Paleolithic rock paintings in a cave in the Dordogne, in southwest France. They have been carbon-dated to 15,000 B.C.

3 WEATHERING

1. Quoted in the *Guardian* article. No original source.

2. Excerpt from "Against Coupling" by Fleur Adcock. In *High Tide in the Garden.* New York: Oxford University Press, 1971.

3. Excerpt from "Tokens" by Fleur Adcock. In *Poems 1960–2000.* Highgreen, Northumberland, England: Bloodaxe Books, 2000.

4. Excerpt from "Love After Love" by Derek Walcott. In *Collected Poems 1948–1984.* New York: Farrar, Straus and Giroux, 1986.

4 SUNSET

1. Excerpt from "Postscript" by Seamus Heaney. In *The Spirit Level.* New York: Farrar, Straus and Giroux, 1996.

2. See *Selected Poems of Rainer Maria Rilke.* Trans. Robert Bly. New York: Harper & Row, 1981.

3. Excerpt from "Little Gidding" by T. S. Eliot. In *Four Quartets*. New York: Harcourt, Inc., 1943.

4. Julian of Norwich (1342–1416) wrote the manuscript *Showing of Love*.

5   FOR THE SAKE OF STRANGERS

1. *Awake* by Dorianne Laux. Rochester, N.Y.: Boa Editions, 1990.

2. *What We Carry* by Dorianne Laux. Rochester, N.Y.: Boa Editions, 1994.

3. *Hannah's Gift* by Maria Housden. New York: Bantam Books, 2002.

4. See *Sacred Journeys in a Modern World* by Roger Housden. New York: Simon and Schuster, 1998.

5. Excerpt from "Wild Geese" by Mary Oliver. In *Dream Work* Boston: Atlantic Monthly, 1986.

6   SONG OF A MAN WHO HAS COME THROUGH

1. *Lady Chatterly's Lover: Complete and Unexpurgated 1928 Orioli Edition* by D. H. Lawrence. New York: Bantam Classics, 1983.

2. Excerpt from "Song of the Open Road" by Walt Whitman. In *Leaves of Grass*. New York: Modern Library, 1993.

3. Excerpt from "Life XX" by Emily Dickinson. In *Complete Poems of Emily Dickinson Part 1*. New York: Little Brown, 1976.

4. Excerpt from a 1915 sonnet by John Masefield (1878–1967). Most collections of his work are no longer in print.

5. Hazrat Inayat Khan (1882–1927) was the founder of the

Sufi Order of the West. He was born into a Muslim family of musicians in India and traveled to America and Europe with the message of the unity of all religions.

6. Excerpt from "To Praise Is the Whole Thing" by Rainer Maria Rilke. In *Selected Poems of Rainer Maria Rilke*. Trans. Robert Bly. New York: Harper & Row, 1981.

7   LYING IN A HAMMOCK AT WILLIAM DUFFY'S FARM IN PINE ISLAND, MINNESOTA

1. *What Should I Do with My Life?* by Po Bronson. New York: Random House, 2002.

2. Excerpt from "A Prayer to Escape the Market Place" by James Wright. In *Above the River: The Complete Poems*. New York: Farrar, Straus and Giroux, 1990.

3. Excerpt from "A Winter Daybreak Above Vence" by James Wright. Ibid.

4. Excerpt from "The Archaic Torso of Apollo" by Rainer Maria Rilke. In *Selected Poems of Rainer Maria Rilke*. Trans. Robert Bly. New York: Harper & Row, 1981.

5. Ted Hughes, quoted in *Staying Alive: Real Poems for Unreal Times*. Ed. Neil Astley. New York: Miramax, 2003.

6. Excerpt from "Personal Helicon" by Seamus Heaney. In *Opened Ground: Selected Poems 1966–1996*. New York: Farrar, Straus and Giroux, 1999.

7. Excerpt from "When Death Comes" by Mary Oliver. In *New and Selected Poems*. Boston: Beacon Press, 1992.

9   THE ART OF DISAPPEARING

1. Excerpt from "Let's Go Home" by Rumi. In *Open Secret.* Trans. Coleman Barks. Boston: Shambhala Publications, 1999.

2. Ray Gatchalian. See dedication to Ray in *Ten Poems to Set You Free.* New York: Harmony Books, 2003.

3. Excerpt from "The Holy Longing" by Goethe. Trans. Robert Bly. From *The Soul Is Here for Its Own Joy.* Ed. Robert Bly. New York: Ecco Press, 1995.

10   THE MIND OF ABSOLUTE TRUTH

1. Excerpt from *Tao Te Ching* by Lao Tzu. Trans. Man-Ho Kwok, Martin Palmer, and Jay Ramsay. New York: Penguin, 1997.

   Lao Tsu was reputed to have lived in China around the beginning of the fifth century B.C., and to have met Confucius, whom he chastised for being attached to power, wealth, and position. The *Tao Te Ching* is in fact a collection of stories and teachings from different sources. The Taoists attributed it to Lao Tsu—who was known in folk memory as a great teacher who stood for a more natural way than Confucius—in order to counter the prevailing Confucian wisdom. Lao Tsu is not even a proper name; it simply means "Old Master."

2. Mahayana Buddhism is the form of Buddhism prevalent in Tibet, China, and Japan. It arose in the first century B.C. as a counter to Theravadan Buddhism, which focused primarily on meditation within a monastic environment. Mahayana (literally, "Greater Vehicle" or "Ox-Cart")

teachings made Buddhism accessible to the general public and emphasized the values of compassion and generosity toward others.

3. See *Long Pilgrimage: The Life and Teachings of the Shivapuri Baba* by J. G. Bennett. Middletown, Cal.: Dawn Horse Press, 1983.

4. Excerpt from *Joseph the lost will return* by Hafez. In *The Soul Is Here for Its Own Joy*. Ed. Robert Bly. New York: Ecco Press, 1995.

5. Excerpt from *Out Beyond Ideas of Wrongdoing* by Rumi. In *The Essential Rumi*, trans. Coleman Barks. San Francisco: HarperSanFrancisco, 1995.

6. Hindu saying quoted as an epigram in *The Ramayana*. Trans. W. S. Buck. Berkeley, Cal.: University of California Press, 1976.

7. Excerpt from "East Coker" by T. S. Eliot. In *The Four Quartets*. New York: Harcourt, Inc., 1943.

11   WHEN DEATH COMES

1. Excerpt from "Love" by Czeslaw Milosz. In *New and Collected Poems 1931–2001*. New York: Ecco Press, 2001.

2. Excerpt from "The Journey" by Mary Oliver. In *New and Selected Poems*. Boston: Beacon Press, 1992.

3. Excerpt from "The Summer Day." Ibid.

Recommended Reading

BILLY COLLINS

Nine Horses: Poems
Picnic, Lightning
Sailing Alone Around the Room: New and Selected Poems

HAYDEN CARRUTH

Doctor Jazz: Poems, 1996–2000
Scrambled Eggs and Whiskey: Poems 1991–1995
The Selected Poetry of Hayden Carruth

FLEUR ADCOCK

High Tide in the Garden
Poems 1960–2000

RAINER MARIA RILKE

Ahead of All Parting: The Selected Poetry and Prose
    of Rainer Maria Rilke (trans. Stephen Mitchell)
Rilke's Book of Hours: Love Poems to God
    (trans. Anita Barrows and Joanna R. Macy)
Selected Poems of Rainer Maria Rilke
    (trans. Robert Bly)

The Selected Poetry of Rainer Maria Rilke
   (trans. Stephen Mitchell)

DORIANNE LAUX

Smoke
The Poet's Companion: A Guide to the Pleasures of Writing Poetry
   (with Kim Addonizio)
What We Carry: Poems

D. H. LAWRENCE

Complete Poems
Any of his novels
Out of Sheer Rage: Wrestling with D. H. Lawrence
   (by Geoff Dyer)

JAMES WRIGHT

Above the River: The Complete Poems

JOHN KEATS

The Complete Poems of John Keats
Selected Poems

NAOMI SHIHAB NYE

19 Varieties of Gazelle: Poems of the Middle East
The Words Under the Words: Selected Poems
This Same Sky: A Collection of Poems from Around the World
   (Editor)

MARY OLIVER

The Leaf and the Cloud: A Poem
New and Selected Poems
West Wind: Poems and Prose Poems
What Do We Know

Other Poets to Last a Lifetime:
A Brief List

T. S. ELIOT
Four Quartets

HAFIZ
The Gift: Poems by Hafiz the Great Sufi Master
  (Trans. Daniel Ladinsky)
The Subject Tonight Is Love: 60 Wild and Sweet Poems of Hafiz
  (trans. Daniel Ladinsky)

ANTONIO MACHADO
Times Alone: Selected Poems of Antonio Machado
  (trans. Robert Bly)

CZESLAW MILOSZ
New and Collected Poems 1931–2001

PABLO NERUDA
*Full Woman, Fleshly Apple, Hot Moon: Selected Poems of Pablo
  Neruda* (trans. Stephen Mitchell)
100 Love Sonnets (trans. Stephen Tapscott)

Twenty Love Poems and a Song of Despair
    (trans. W. S. Merwin)

RUMI
The Essential Rumi (trans. Coleman Barks)
The Soul of Rumi (trans. Coleman Barks)

WILLIAM SHAKESPEARE
The Sonnets

WALT WHITMAN
Leaves of Grass

WILLIAM WORDSWORTH
The Prelude
Selected Poetry of William Wordsworth

Acknowledgments

As always, my thanks go first and foremost to the poets, eleven of them, whose work has made this volume possible. Second, to my sterling editor, Toinette Lippe, for all her careful attention and also for the many ways in which she has treated this entire series as a labor of love. Then, to my agent, Kim Witherspoon, who safely shepherded this book through the shoals of the contract; to Shaye Areheart, whose support as publisher has been invaluable throughout; and to Mary Schuck, without whose inspired jacket designs the series would have been much the poorer. Finally, to all those readers who have found inspiration and value in the earlier Ten Poems books, and whose interest has spawned this fourth and final volume.

Permissions

Grateful acknowledgment is made to the following for permission to reprint previously published material:

Beacon Press: "When Death Comes" from *New and Selected Poems* by Mary Oliver. Copyright © 1992 by Mary Oliver. Reprinted by permission of Beacon Press, Boston.

Bloodaxe Books: "Weathering" and an excerpt from "Against Coupling" from *Poems 1960–2000* by Fleur Adcock. Copyright © 2000 by Fleur Adcock. Reprinted by permission of Bloodaxe Books.

BOA Editions, Ltd.: "For the Sake of Strangers" from *What We Carry* by Dorianne Laux. Copyright © 1984 by Dorianne Laux. Reprinted by permission of BOA Editions, Ltd.

Copper Canyon Press: "Ecstasy" from *Scrambled Eggs & Whiskey: Poems 1991–1995* by Hayden Carruth. Copyright © 1996 by Hayden Carruth. Reprinted by permission of Copper Canyon Press, Box 271, Port Townsend, WA 98368.

Farrar, Straus and Giroux, LLC.: Excerpt from "Postscript" from *Opened Ground: Selected Poems 1966–1996* by Seamus Heaney. Copyright © 1998 by Seamus Heaney. Reprinted by permission of Farrar, Straus and Giroux, LLC.

About the Author

Roger Housden, a native of Bath, England, emigrated to the United States in 1998. He now lives in New York City with his wife, Maria. His books explore the existential and spiritual issues of our time. His most recent works include *Ten Poems to Set You Free, Risking Everything: 110 Poems of Love and Revelation, Ten Poems to Open Your Heart, Chasing Rumi: A Fable About Finding the Heart's True Desire,* and *Ten Poems to Change Your Life.* He gives a small number of individual coaching sessions by phone on the transformational power of poetry and the life themes covered in the Ten Poems series. You can email him at tenpoems@juno.com.